I0438833

The Man

in the

Desert

Diary of a Freed Addict

The Man

in the

Desert

Diary of a Freed Addict

by

Tom Lomas

ISBN 1-58500-880-X
Published in association with Freedom Ministries, Inc.
Cover by Chris Lomas

*"Faith and reason are like two wings on which the human
spirit rises to the contemplation of truth."*
(Pope John Paul II - 1998 Encyclical Letter)

"What a wonderful discovery is the way of the Lord."
(*40 Days to Freedom* - Day 39)

TABLE OF CONTENTS

From 1990 to 1992, I wrote a book entitled *40 Days to Freedom*. Immediately before the writing started, I had been healed from an addiction to sexual lust which had its roots in my discovery of pornography as a youngster and persisted and grew worse until, at age fifty, I was totally and irrevocably freed through a God-given procedure hidden in the Gospels of the New Testament. I say hidden because, having been a Christian all my life and having been very familiar with the specific scripture involved, never before, to my knowledge, had its true meaning been revealed, not by any *Bible* teacher, nor by any priest or minister. This truth is so powerful it is capable of solving all of the problems and challenges of a world filled with greed and lust and conflict. I will leave the details of this miraculous procedure for later in this work.

About a month after the healing, I was directed to write *40 Days to Freedom* about the procedure so the same healing I had received could be experienced by others suffering from all sorts of addictions, harmful obsessions, and compulsive behavior. Not to be included in that first writing was my testimony or life story about my addiction and healing.

Immediately after completion of the first manuscript, a door opened to prison ministry; and I saw this as a calling for giving my verbal testimony of healing and for distributing the book which was to be published in early 1995. In the years following we have been wonderfully blessed to have witnessed, in some instances first-hand, many healings and many souls freed to a new life of peace and fulfillment. Some of the testimonies of those blessed with this true freedom are reported in various locations at our web site (www.40days2freedom.org). I have been asked many times if I would write another book; and I would usually respond that the distribution of the one book would be a full-time job for the rest of my life which seems to be the opposite of inspiration for this new work.

After a year part-time, our ministry, Freedom Ministries,

Inc., was called full-time in early 1996. At that time, I received three key messages or directions: "(1) the organized churches are filled with people in bondage who are not receiving from their churches what they need to break their chains; (2) this message of freedom (contained in *40 Days to Freedom* and this new work) will blanket the earth; (3) distribute the books and I'll (God) take care of the rest." These were received, not together, but within a time frame of a week.

While the prison doors have flown open to us, the church doors have not. This is not a criticism but a simple fact. For the most part, when we have ministered at churches, the invitation has not come from clergy or pastors, but from members within the congregation or lay ministries within the church. In each instance, our verbal testimony and the free distribution of our first book have had a powerful impact. And we have been able to reach both the churched and unchurched through the Internet (since early 1996) and through prison ministries, prison chaplains, and recovery ministries. Through early 1999, sixteen thousand seven hundred copies of *40 Days to Freedom* have been distributed throughout the USA and twenty-three other countries.

The third message told me I was to do no fund raising for our legal charity. No special money raising events, no big sales pitches, rather making the opportunity to donate or invest in God's work quietly available. I was being led to be a messenger, not a fund-raiser; and I was shown the two are not compatible in the same person.

Since most of those we were serving were not people of material means, after my savings were exhausted with the second printing of *40 Days to Freedom* in early 1998, our ministry remained financially lean (broke) to the present time. Somehow, the bills were always paid. More specifics on this later.

We knew there would be a third printing of *40 Days to Freedom* and we knew it would be fifty thousand copies; but, with the ministry checking account averaging under five hundred dollars, we didn't know how. We simply trusted God as we are encouraged to do throughout the *Bible*.

Early one morning in May 1999, while in study and prayer in my office, I was given the title *The Man in the Desert*. It was the final piece to a puzzle that started with the writing of *40 Days to Freedom*; and in a rush all of the pieces came flying together. I was to write this new book, which would include my life's testimony, which would provide the funding to continue the free flow of *40 Days to Freedom* to the prisons and jails and ministries where the need is so great and the resources so sparse.

More importantly, *The Man in the Desert*, through its own message, would become an important part of God's "blanketing the earth" with His message of freedom to all His children regardless of their earthly circumstances.

This work on the salvation of the real person, the inner person, the soul, is the true story of three men, each in his own desert, solitary, individual, which each must be, whether he is one of a starving multitude in Africa or a participant in the so-called fruits of the affluent in America. We each have our own walk through our earth-life no matter how short or how long. Each is an individual and, in a sense, alone in our decisions and reactions to life's challenges, though along the way we may be influenced by others, as we are all alone and apart from other earth-bound mortals when we have breathed our last and depart for, what most truly consider, the vast unknown. We will attempt here to make that unknown known so the reader will see departing the earth-life as a simple transition to a better life, the life for which he was created. The reader will see the true importance of the earth-life as a preparation for that to come.

Each individual consists of the inner person, the real person, often masked from others, and the outer person which we display to others. We may not know the inner person as well as we think. For example we may believe the inner person is a monster, particularly if we are trapped in addiction where we have lost the ability to make certain decisions, important decisions, life-affecting decisions. We may better know the outer person, the one we pretend to be, the one we would like to be while our view of the inner person may be impeded by guilt or an unwillingness to face the truth. My perception may be clouded. In fact, anyone trapped in addiction or habitual sin cannot fully see the truth.

This opens a potential paradox where Jesus told us we would know the truth and the truth would set us free; but he also said the people he was instructing had eyes that could not see and ears that could not hear. So how can we see and know the truth and become free if we can't see or hear the truth? This very important question is answered in the following pages.

Any person who believes he is a monster is buying a lie. No

matter how gross the behavior, the real person cannot be other than a beautiful, unique masterpiece from the Master Creator. Freedom from this clouded, perverted vision is available to every person, freedom to see with the eyes of Jesus, to know his peace, his joy, his harmony with all of creation. The way to this freedom is presented for all to use within these pages.

For the purpose of our presentation, the word addiction will refer to anything which has control over us and over which we have little or no control. In addition to the obvious this would include anger, judgmentalism, unforgiveness, arrogance, self-centeredness, anything in the realm of harmful, controlling obsession which is opposed to unselfish love. Please also be aware, though the writer is a man and reports on his personal experience with one addiction more prevalent with men than women, most of what is said pertains to all addictions, harmful obsessions, and habitual sin.

Since we are here defining terms, any reference to *sin* will point to that which is out of harmony with God, who is *love*, and His immutable laws. The term *God* will refer to the Creator of the universe and all in it with the exception of that created by man. *God, Creator, Almighty,* and *Father* refer to the same Being. He could equally be referred to as *Mother*; but, since we are writing from a male perspective, please forgive the excessive use of that gender in this work. It is our prayer that women will find here material useful for overcoming their own challenges in life as well as information helpful to the men they love.

The inner and outer persons may be in conflict or in harmony with each other, which will play an important part in the agony or joy of the individual, both in this world and the next. An example of conflicting personalities would be Dr. Jekyll and Mr. Hyde. Perhaps the prime example of the two being in harmony would be Jesus of Nazareth or, in modern times, Mother Teresa. If we are to attain peace and joy both in this life and the next, then this harmony is not only desirable but necessary. Our Father Creator has provided two ways to achieve this harmony; and both were disclosed by Jesus during his earthly sojourn. This was his reference when he told us that he is the way and the truth and the life. One of the two ways is easier and more fulfilling than the other; however, most people choose the harder way. Why? This too we will explore.

We hope and it is our intent that the message of *The Man in the Desert* will be a source of freedom from bondage from all sorts of enslavement for people all over the world including freedom from fear of the unknown. We were created, every one of us, to be free, to make our own choices, our own decisions. We were each equipped with an inner voice, an inner knowledge of our Father Creator, an *Internal Bible* to guide us through our lives.

Almost from the moment of our birth, forces, both human and spiritual, endeavor to bury and recreate in their image that internal operating system which is a gift from a loving Father. That inner knowledge can only be stifled for a time; ultimately, as Jesus told us, we will all know the truth and we will all be free. Free from what? From lies and deceit. The truth is wonderful and nothing to fear. And to live the way of the truth is not a sacrifice for we are not required to give up anything worthwhile. Living the truth, to the outside world, can appear to be a sacrifice; but this writer has experienced a peace and contentment he had never before known and the true meaning of "my yoke is easy and my burden light."

We might add that what we present here, in addition to our life story, is what we have learned about God from God. While our ministry has been materially poor in the eyes of the world and we have given our all to obey God's direction through that ministry, we have already been rewarded far beyond anything we could have anticipated or imagined. This included our prison ministry experience starting with our first of many visits to those incarcerated at Lake Correctional Institution in Clermont, Florida, in 1992, and many other prisons and jails since. In fact our reward has been beyond counting and one that we will take with us when we depart this short stay on earth.

God has used many sources in His teaching, some orthodox or conventional and some very unorthodox that may even be judged as heresy by those who profess that only by proclaiming the blood of Christ can we enter through the gates of heaven. Here we will present the true meaning of the awesome sacrifice Jesus made which is not rooted in pagan ritual of old and which does not require that we believe in a God of vengeance and anger and wrath. Well, we can relax, as our Father will be merciful with our wayward accusers as well as the rest of us who can no longer swallow the legends and myths as facts, the same myths which contribute to the violence of our world today. We count ourselves in good company as even Jesus was accused of being a devil and Joan of Arc a heretic by the narrow-minded of their times.

On this issue of being saved, I will never forget hearing a Protestant minister on radio express that there are four categories of saved or unsaved people. The first is those who know they are saved and are saved. The second is those who know they are not saved who are not saved. Pretty orthodox so far until we get to the third which is those, who know they are saved, who are not saved, and the fourth which is those, who do not know they are saved, who are saved. Please remember, this is not my speculation but was heard on a Christian radio station spoken by an ordained Protestant minister. I emphasize general denomination since Roman Catholics no longer profess that only Christians are to enter heaven. I accepted this information as knowledge of God from God.

Much of what He has taught me would be considered far more radical than this by mainstream Christianity; and some I initially rejected based on my background as a somewhat orthodox, cradle Catholic. But, when God tweaked my *Internal Bible*, I would return to His teaching to find His truth not religion's. Not that I rejected all orthodox teaching; but, with my healing from addiction in 1990, I was given what, at that time, I could only call the eyes of Jesus which have allowed me to discern what is of God and what is of man. More on this to come later.

We pray that the reader will enter this text with a seeking, open mind and an open heart, that he or she will be filled with the peace and knowledge that comes from the truth, and that he

or she will be guided by that inner voice which comes from the
source of all truth.

I. THE FIRST FIFTY YEARS

The First Man

As a young child, my life would have appeared normal to most folks. At age three, my family bought their first home in the suburbs of Worcester, Massachusetts. There were four of us, in addition to Mother and Dad was my brother Bob who was thirteen years older than I. I can't remember much from those early years; but I do remember that Bob loved me a lot. I remember he and his buddies taking me mostly riding on Bob's shoulders, for what seemed like miles, to Montrose's for ice cream. He teased me, he loved me, he spoiled me, and I loved him.

But I loved Mother, then Mummy, the best. She was thirty-eight when I was born. I learned later there was one miscarriage between Bob and me. She was beautiful, with long wavy dark hair and I hugged her and kissed her all the time, even in public. She was full of life and ambition.

Bob left home to join the occupation forces of World War II in Europe when I was five and it seemed most of my family affection, if not all, then came from my mother. She was also the source of all my discipline which I later saw as love.

My father was a passive man. I mostly remember him taking Mummy and me to the movies every week in those early years; and we would go for drives in the country on Sundays, sometimes to apple orchards or other points of interest. Otherwise, I didn't have much contact with him. I knew he loved me; but I guess I didn't really feel it. He pretty much left the running of the family to Mummy. Later, when I became a father, I learned to appreciate the role and its challenge.

Once in a while, not often, my parents would have verbal fights followed by seemingly endless periods of silence. That I hated. When they made up, which they always would, I was happy. I truly don't remember who would apologize first; but, realizing my mother's assertive nature, I'm sure it was usually Dad.

Puberty and Sexual Enlightenment?

The remainder of my young years until puberty were unremarkable. I was a good boy, staying out of trouble, and would avoid rather than seek fights. My school work was above average; but I never made any honor roles until later in college when I was paying for my education. I found out about sex from my friends and discovered pornography at an early age.

Strangely, while I consciously loved my mother more than any other person, according to a psychiatrist who counseled me in 1968, I saw my mother usurping my father's role, robbing him of his manhood, and I therefore developed a subconscious hate for and fear of all women which manifested in a sexual addiction. Masturbation and pornography were frequent companions. I will not discuss all the manifestations of this plague; but I had several. For purpose of disclosure to the reader, I will say that my lust was directed at sexually mature females. Further, by the grace of God, I never physically accosted anyone; nor have I ever been incarcerated except for the imprisonment of my mind. You see, the addict is not in control. In the beginning of the addiction he won't admit it. He initially takes the bait. It's as if the temptation is saying, "Oh, come on. You need a break. You've been under a lot of pressure. So what if it's a sin. You're only human. God will forgive you. You won't get hooked." These lies he buys over and over until he's owned, all wrapped up in chains with a big padlock. Then the lies change: "Look at yourself! You're out of control! You're a monster, an embarrassment to everyone in your life! You're going to get caught! Why don't you do yourself and everyone else a favor and commit suicide? Just end it!"

Only someone who has walked in the shoes of the addict can understand how helpless, how lost he is. There is no cure, save one. Oh, sure, secular methods will help to control the manifestations with some; but the internal battle continues. The addict is sentenced to life in the prison of his own mind unless he takes the one path to the one source of freedom.

Many young men grow out of their sexual hang-ups as they

grow into manhood and establish careers and families; many don't. With some, as myself, the hang-up intensifies and become a full-blown, controlling addiction, becomes the single most important thing in the addict's life. Now, the addict is not aware of this because he is deceived. He believes he's still in control and in fact will never blame the addiction for his problems. Quite the opposite, when problems are confronted, he will run to the addiction for comfort or escape which, of course, worsens his problem whatever it may be.

Through high school, I was, in the opinion of some, a good-looking, clean-cut boy. Only I was aware of the demon that lived within me; though I was unaware of its full danger. I had girlfriends, went on dates, was a good dancer. Since mine was the Class of '57, I experienced the birth of rock-and-roll and, of course, Elvis was my favorite. During my high school years, I knew most of his songs by heart. Though I enjoyed sports, I was a non-athlete, and was never one of the elite or more popular kids. The comments by my class yearbook picture were: "Always smiling ..... butch haircut ...... deep voice .... good dancer."

Aviation Cadet Training

After my fascination with Randolph Scott, the cowboy movie star, ended before entering puberty, I determined I would be a jet fighter pilot when I grew up. This commitment continued into young-manhood. My last year in high school and both years, while attending Worcester Junior College, I applied for acceptance to the Air Force Academy in Colorado Springs. In that final year I made it to number six on Senator John F. Kennedy's list of nominees; but only the top two were accepted. But my tests and applications were not in vain as I was accepted for Air Force Pilot Aviation Cadet Training.

Having never been further south than New Jersey, I was truly thrilled, after graduating cum laude from junior college, to be hopping on an airliner to San Antonio. My delight ended abruptly, when upon stepping from the bus at Lackland Air Force Base, "Cage them eyeballs, Mister!" was screamed at me by a young man in uniform about two inches from me, nose-to-nose. My only previous military experience was less than two years as a Boy Scout.

My next few months as a fourth-class Aviation Cadet was a living hell but good preparation for something later on that would save my life. Here I learned to live one day at a time. The discipline was such a shock and created such misery that each night as our lights were turned off; and, finally, I could have a little peace, I prayed to God to help me survive just one more day. If we couldn't take it, we were allowed to write a letter of self elimination which meant we could reenter civilian life after serving two years on enlisted status. Not only my dream but also my pride would not allow that.

Military life agreed with me and somewhat limited my indulgence in my addiction. Soon, I was an upper-classman and was likewise feared by the new arrivals as I vented my need to retaliate. I particularly remember one meal. Every item at one's place setting had to be perfectly placed or "gigged" in alignment with every other item. The unfortunate lower-classman sitting beside me for the meal was mercilessly hazed by me for the entire meal and certainly left hungry. I later learned he had been a very able heavy-weight wrestler in college and probably could have easily broken skinny me in two. I soon realized attracting the hate of others is not the path to effective leadership. As a second-class, upper-classman I became drill team commander for Dog Squadron. As you might suspect, Dog Squadron Drill Team had never won a competition. Certainly the high point of my cadet days was when it did under my command.

After about a year of basic officer training, several of my buddies and I headed for the small town of Bartow in Central Florida where we entered the initial phase of our flight training. Two important things happened while I was stationed at Bartow Air Base. With the first my world ended. I washed out of pilot training which left me in a void. This was something I never considered to be possible. It seemed the cockpit and I were not compatible, at least not compatible enough to satisfy my instructor, so I was one of three hundred sixty two cadets, out of a class of four hundred fifty, to "bite the dust."

I was given two options neither of which I found desirable. I could enter the initial flight training phase of Navigator Aviation Cadets where I could win those second lieutenant gold bars on schedule; but the silver wings would be those of a navigator which, at the time, I considered undesirable. My other option was to serve two years on enlisted status before I would be able to leave the military; or I could still have career opportunity. I sought the counsel of the base chaplain who advised me to choose the navigator training option. His logic was, if I didn't like it, I would still be able to write the letter of self-elimination which would then trigger the enlisted-and-out choice. Since these were my only choices, I could not argue with his logic and followed his advice which proved sound.

I Meet Pat

The second important occurrence of my Bartow tenure was quite the opposite of the first as I met the woman who was to become my wife. One evening some of the other cadets in similar circumstance to mine decided to head for the Florida Southern College Campus, a short drive away, to do some girl watching; and I was invited to go along.

A small digression here to the earlier reference to Dr. Jekyll and Mr. Hyde is necessary. As with the good doctor, there is a normal, healthy person within the addict struggling for supremacy over the evil Mr. Hyde. Every one of us has to face this struggle to one degree or another. This is both the blessing and the curse of free will. And our Creator refuses to manipulate that free will. If he did, we would all just be a bunch of puppets automatically responding to the controls of the puppet-master.

The *Bible* tells us we were created by God to be His friends. Friendship, true friendship, loving friendship is a choice. It cannot be manipulated. It cannot be forced. This would be contrary to the nature of God, contrary to the nature of love. At this point in my life, in my internal battle between good and evil, the good side was still dominant most of the time. The point I'm trying to make is that the young man walking the sidewalks of the Florida Southern Campus was still capable of falling in love

5

with the young woman he met that evening in 1960. And he did.

Three young men walking met two young women walking. I was immediately taken with Pat. She had an air of humility coupled with a smile which caused my heart to smile. And her voice created a music within me I had not experienced before.

At this time I was awaiting transfer back to Texas for navigator training, so our courtship was brief, a matter of weeks; but I popped the question and she accepted. I still had a year remaining before completion of training and receiving my commission as a second lieutenant. We wrote frequently; but had only two visits during that year. One was during a very brief stop-over at MacDill Air Force Base during a training mission from Texas to Bermuda. The other was during the Christmas holiday of 1960 when I was able to take some leave and visit for a few days.

Our romance survived our separation; and our love for each other grew. Pat's personality being the opposite of my mother's was a definite attraction to me. I seemed to inherit my mother's dominant, assertive nature; and the combination, which with us was the opposite of my folks, seemed to work. We married in April of 1961 without having known each other sexually. This intimacy I share for a reason. Though masturbation and lust were my frequent companions, my religious upbringing had taught me that sexual intercourse before marriage was wrong. And, though Pat did not have the religious background, she did have a strong moral code and a strong personal will-power.

We were not sexually compatible; and this resulted in obvious problems in our marriage; and became my excuse for indulgence in my addiction. At the time, I did not see the true reason for our incompatibility, which was my addiction; and this is characteristic of every addiction. The addict is willing to blame everyone else and everything else for his problems but never the addiction. He sees his addiction as the escape from his problems; and, I might at this point add, he doesn't recognize, in fact refuses to recognize, that he's addicted. He runs to his addiction to escape from his world of problems, becomes more addicted, his problems grow, he runs to his addiction, his problems grow, he is out of control. This is the destructive cycle of every addiction; and the objective of every addiction is the alienation of the addict from everything that is good, from everything that is of God, to stimulate pride and greed and lust and over-indulgence and fulfillment of self at the expense of others, no matter what, until it destroys the addict, bodily, spiritually, any way it can. Death is the objective of every addiction.

Addiction Rules

Again, we are referring to addiction as anything that controls us, imprisons us, where we have little or no control. In the sex addiction arena alone, a psychologist, who counseled me in the late eighties, estimated that better than half of all men have sexual hang-ups of one kind or another. If we add to sexual hang-ups, overeating, substance abuse, fear, depression, money, power, judgmentalism, anger, religious dogma, and on and on, what do we have? A world of addicts? Almost! Impossible situation? Not! Not since this addict found total freedom, a freedom so wonderful, it's even worth the personal price of the addiction.

Society has created many myths to feed our addictions. It will tell us we must learn if we are sexually compatible before marriage to avoid having a bad marriage as if sex was the most important aspect of marriage. This is far from the truth as love, not lust, unselfish, giving, forgiving is the most important aspect of marriage. I believe with every marriage the sex aspect will be rewarding, if not fulfilling, as long as the love is true and greed and lust and pride are kept out of the relationship. Of course we, as humans, cannot do this; but God can through us. Just look at what He accomplished living through the man named Jesus. He does this with every healthy marriage whether we recognize it or not. If we allow Him to live through us, nothing is impossible.

My addiction, though I truly loved Pat, polluted our marriage as I was too filled with self. This too is true with every addiction. There is the tendency to focus on self rather than other which has become the way of our entire society. If this were not so, there would be no lies, no greed, no abortion, no

7

crime, no wars, no death penalty, etc. Would this require returning to the day of the caveman? Not at all! We would not only be more loving but more clear minded, more innovative, and more productive. If we were a society focused on all others as brothers and sisters under our one Father, there would be no weapons; and, instead of reaching for planets, we would be reaching for stars.

Addiction Infects All Aspects of Life

The addiction also affected every other aspect of my life as a father, as a provider, as a military officer, as a Catholic Christian, and as a participant in society. With the addiction, the lust compulsion, always in the front of my mind, I was always less than I was capable of being. He, who is free from habitual sin, is free to allow God to flow through him and become all he is capable of being in every endeavor in his life without effort, without struggle. He becomes in harmony with God and His universe and simply flows freely. This is what we see when we see a Gandhi, a Mother Teresa, a Joan of Arc, a Jesus of Nazareth. It seems to the world that these outstanding people achieve the impossible; but their "yoke is easy and their burden light." In each case they freely gave of self, hanging on to nothing but God, trusting Him only for their direction, against all odds. "If God be for me, who can be against me?" Only the enemy of God, which is the opposite of God, only the force of evil, which has no power unless we give in to it, can be against me.

The enemy, God's enemy, our enemy, was created by man and can be destroyed by man allowing God to flow through man. "Be perfect as your heavenly Father is perfect." God makes man perfect. Man creates imperfection by going against God. So it has been since the first man. So it will continue until man surrenders to the freedom of allowing God to live in and through him until man is "born again."

The demon possession of the twentieth century is addiction or habitual sin. The ultimate freedom of man is experienced by being born again. Surrendering to God is not giving up freedom like surrendering to the world and its ways of pride and greed and lust. The freedom of the world is a facade, is deceit, is the opposite of freedom, is bondage.

Surrendering to God is seeking His Divine Love to enter our soul, our internal being, and work through our life. This is not a confining love, a possessing love, but is a giving love, a forgiving love, being free to hold on to nothing but God Himself, seeking, allowing Him to take residence within our souls and to express Himself, His love, through us. Yet, though we surrender and seek oneness with Him, to achieve this He will never imprison, will never take away our freedom to turn away from Him, until we enter His domain, His Celestial Heaven, when, through our choice, our seeking, and His response, we experience our final transformation, exchanging our mind for His mind, our will for His will, and become His Divine Angel.

Air Force Career

Though I was imprisoned by my lust demon I was performing well in the eyes of the world and in my career in the world. I was promoted early to the rank of first lieutenant which allowed my early advancement from the right seat as a navigator of the B-52G to the left seat as radar-navigator or bombardier in older Air Force terminology.

There are three teams flying this indomitable, still air-born, flying wonder. Behind the pilot team and facing to the rear is the defense team consisting of the electronic warfare officer (EWO) and gunner who had remote control of his weapon through television and radar, a substantial progression from the WWII days where the gunners were stationed throughout the aircraft firing their machine guns by hand.

The job of the EWO was to jam enemy radar and to prevent successful missile attack against our aircraft and its deadly cargo. Which brings me to what I had considered the most important team, facing forward on the lower deck, the offense team. The navigator would direct the aircraft toward the intended target and the radar-navigator would fly the craft for the last leg over the target and dispense the bomb or bombs. I was thoroughly dedicated to the completion of my mission which could have meant the destruction of many lives. I had accepted, that should we experience nuclear war, my family, which I would leave behind to fly my deadly mission, would be unlikely to survive and my retaliation would be justified.

Though I served during the Cuban Missile Crisis and the Viet Nam Era, I never saw combative action as the specialty of my squadron was the Cold War and its deterrent. The major world powers of that time each knew the starting of such a conflict would mean mutual destruction which resulted in a standoff that succeeded. The world of today is different where retaliatory power alone is unlikely to stop a fanatical aggressor bent on a holy war. The writer believes this to be the more dangerous of the two worlds and that another answer to this world-ending threat is needed. That answer will be addressed in later chapters.

Military Outcast to Branded Civilian

During our Air Force career, I was not free. My personal demon, my Mr. Hyde, grew in power and control until, in 1968, there was an incident of exhibitionism which changed everything in my and my family's life in this world. Indeed, it changed our world. After almost a year of counseling by a psychiatrist, my family and I were ejected from the military into the civilian world of "dog eat dog" as characterized by a friend and relative.

My older brother, who didn't have my formal education, was financially more successful than I as a salesman of insurance and inspired me to give sales a try. But there was a problem. Though I had never been incarcerated, my military career termination hindered my being accepted for employment. Interview after interview, I had to explain "why." Interview after interview, I would return to my car feeling like a broken animal, breaking into tears as I slumped behind the steering wheel, sobbing, "Please, God, please don't make me have to explain that again!"

Finally I found a man, who owned his own insurance and investment agency, who was willing to take a chance on me. The psychiatrist, though he had diagnosed "classic neurosis" which progressed into a "masterful instinct," had pronounced to the Air Force that, in his opinion, I was now "in control" and able to "resume my full military duties." The Air Force fired me anyway. But the man, who was to become my mentor, saw something in me that caused him to hire me, to take a chance. Though I was far from cured, I was enough in control of my compulsion that his decision didn't backfire on him. I had a wife and three small children to support. This was my motivation to succeed in the new career of insurance and investment sales; and, with my mentor's guidance and hard work and dedication, I did succeed. In fact, I became national sales champion for a medium-sized insurance company.

After a few years in my new career, our fourth child was born; and my family and I were better off in the eyes of the world than we had been when I was a flying captain in the Air Force. This caused a reassessment on my part. How was this possible? When I had left the military, it was under a condition of extreme embarrassment and shame. In the last year before my parting, though I was no longer flying, I was assigned to scheduling and training where I confronted my former associates daily. I was subjected to a trial procedure which had resulted in a discharge under honorable conditions which is one step below an honorable discharge. I had been an officer who was considered to have unlimited potential in my career; and I had blown it.

Now, here I was, just a few years later, national sales champion. Pat and I had bought our first home, a new home. Our children were attending a Catholic school. I was earning far more than I had in the military; yet before 1968, I had never sold anything, much less an intangible. I had been an introvert; but I had changed; and I liked the change in my more outward personality.

The Power of Prayer

How was it possible that my family and I had not only survived the living hell of my creation; but we had prospered? I realized there could be only one answer, that God had given me the strength to overcome and survive and prosper. I immediately felt guilty as I had been short-changing God. I had not been

11

practicing the religion of my birth and raising. From the depths of my soul, in sincere appreciation, I prayed, "God I want to make you first in my life; but I don't know how to do it. I'll start by attending daily mass, Lord; and I'll leave the rest to you. You open the doors you want me to walk through; and I'll do my best to walk through them."

The doors have never stopped opening since that prayer. God will answer the heartfelt prayer of a sinner who is still in sin, as I was, for I was still dominated by sexual lust. Oh sure, there would be occasions when my sin would almost seem dormant when I was strongly focused on God; but it would always come back and my struggle against my compulsion would continue; and its pollution of my life would continue. But I had opened my heart to God and He had responded and He proved not only tolerant but patient.

The words of the prayer, I am convinced, were not mine; but were created by God's Spirit as He saw my heart. This is so important because a sincere mind is not enough to effectively communicate with God. Our desire and sincerity must come from the center of our soul, our spiritual heart. This is what Jesus meant when He told us the most important commandment is to "love God with all our heart and all our soul and all our mind and all our strength." Important for who? For us!

We can't fool God with an insincere prayer and expect an answer. He can't be conned. But even if our prayer is not in accord with His will, if it is given in love and heart-felt sincerity, it will be answered. And, if we, at the time, are other than in His will, He will patiently orchestrate a change in us, without trampling our will, through His gentle persuasion, which will answer our true prayer of love to Him which is always to seek oneness with Him as His child, as His son, as His daughter.

Cursillo Involvement

This prayer was the beginning of my life as an apostolic Christian, having a personal relationship with God, and, through that relationship, bringing others to Him. I was soon noticed by others attending daily mass and invited to a Cursillo weekend. This is a movement of lay Catholic Christians which started in

Spain during World War II and has now spread to many denominations. The first Cursillo Retreat occurred in a prison in Majorca where two prisoners were soon to be executed. The local chaplain was unable to reach them as they indulged in gambling and pornography in their final hours. In desperation the chaplain was led to contact the lay leader of a new movement of Christian men which itself was struggling to find momentum.

The leader and a second member from the new Cursillo movement entered the prison trusting God to overcome their initial fears. They shared their testimonies of the new life they had found through Christ and the good news of the Gospel of Jesus and prayed with the prisoners. By dawn on the day of their executions, both had accepted Christ into their hearts. The lay leader asked a special favor of the condemned men. Surprised, they wondered what they could possibly do when they were just moments away from their deaths. They were asked to be intercessors with God to help the new Cursillo Movement get off the ground and be an instrument of God for freeing souls.

Since that day in the forties, Cursillo has spread over our globe and many millions of people, as this writer, have been blessed through the agape (unselfish) love found during the retreat and nourished through the organized fellowship made available to every candidate after his or her weekend experience.

Until the late seventies, I was very active in Cursillo, in my church, and in my community. All of these activities were examples of love, of giving myself to others, of being an instrument used to spread God's love. I was living the commandment of loving as I had been loved. I had again become a pillar in my community as in the Air Force, though there it had been mostly job related and somewhat less family and social. Now the job, family, and social aspects were again present but they were all enhanced by the spiritual. Of the three aspects of our lives, family, social including work, and spiritual, this is the most important. The right relationship with God, not necessarily through religion, will have a positive impact on the other parts of our life. And I was endeavoring to instill the spiritual values in my family, both with the children and with Pat.

Though baptized in a Protestant Church, Pat had little in the way of spirituality before our marriage; and then what I would characterize as typical go-along with your luke-warm husband's religion until I became involved in Cursillo. Then she liked what she saw and was attracted to it, to God; but, at the same time, she was scared. Pat had always been an introvert, a home-body. Now she saw her husband going off to give speeches to win souls to Christ. But her attraction to God was stronger than her fear of social exposure. She became baptized and confirmed Catholic and made her first communion at a Cursillo home mass.

Pat came out of her shell and radiated the love of Christ everywhere she went. And, yes, she even gave speeches in her Cursillo involvement. She had always been a good wife and perfect mother and now she was also participating in the great commission of spreading the good news of God's love for His children. To her husband, her beauty seemed angelic. These were certainly the best years of our marriage when God was at the center of our marriage and of our family.

My business life was also enhanced by the increased spirituality in home and church. I entered management and, as in sales, was also a success. We bought a motor home which was used primarily for vacations with our children. For a month each summer we would cover as many as eight thousand miles exploring our great country. From all appearances, the Lomases were living the good life and had it all together.

Addiction and Hypocrisy

Now, you might reasonably, at this point, accuse me of hypocrisy. Here I appeared to be Mr. All-American, Apostolic Christian, success-in-career, wonderful family man who was a leader in his church and community. While, at the same time, I was this lustful creature who couldn't look at a woman without mentally undressing her and worse. Even if the words of the *Bible* didn't tell us that sins of the mind and heart are real, we would know it. Our *Internal Bible*, our conscience, would tell

14

us. Certainly I felt like a hypocrite with the guilt and the fear of discovery constantly lurking. And even though I had not yet entered the real self-condemnation phase of my addiction, the conflict between what I saw as the two sides of me was taking its toll. But this was not hypocrisy. Above everything else, every human being is a creation of God, a child of God; and God doesn't create monsters but does, as the *Bible* tells us, create only that which is "good."

In fact God is more our parent than our biological parents because He alone created our soul which is the real person whom He created for only one purpose, to live in friendship with Him forever, every soul, no exceptions. So each person is a beautiful unique creation, the very highest creation, of the Master Creator of the universe. Each person is a masterpiece of infinite beauty and cannot be otherwise. All that our Father creates is good.

So, as with the good Dr. Jekyll and the evil Mr. Hyde of his creation, so it was with me. I was the sincere, good person, husband, father, Catholic Christian, worker-provider, giver to my church and community. But I had also created, unintentionally, a monster. The monster was not me but lived within me; and, as with the good Dr. Jekyll, the monster stole my freedom by controlling my thoughts, my mind, imprisoned me, stole my God-given, precious gift of free-will.

How many of us have such a monster living within our souls, feeding us lies, lies that we are not worthy to relate to God, not worthy to relate to good people? How many of us have bought these lies and see ourselves as other than the precious, loved creation we are? How many of us are carrying such burdens?

This, beloved, is the reason Jesus came to earth, to remove these burdens, to set the captives free, by his example and through his Father's strength and very presence within each of us, literally God a part of our being after our rebirth. For He will not force himself on us, will not invade our precious gift of free-will even when that will is no longer controlled by us but by the monster of our creation. We still must, out of the depths of

15

our slavery, choose to accept the freedom He offers. And, make no mistake, if we choose it, if we long for it with our entire being and turn to Him, as our strength to overcome, He will set us free!

At this point, I was still a long way from my freedom; and, even though I had been powerfully and positively impacted by God through Cursillo, I was not yet reborn. With some the rebirthing process takes longer than with others; and with some it can happen in an instant. I believe factors such as the severity and depth of control of the addiction and the totality of surrender to God and His will can affect the speed of our rebirth, of our recovery. What? Could it be the will of God that we suffer. No! However, He will not interfere with our suffering against our will; and it can be and often is our will that we suffer. This again stems from our false image that we are unworthy creatures which can be exacerbated by religion. God's will is that we have peace and joy in the midst of adversity and that we grow through overcoming by using His strength instead of ours. This He portrayed in our role model, Jesus of Nazareth.

Change

In the late seventies, I left my mentor for a full-time management job with a large company. In addition Pat and I sold the house we believed we had outgrown; and we moved to a larger home several miles away, far enough for an excuse to reduce, then stop our Cursillo activity. Gradually, we both became less God-focused and more world- focused. My world still included my addiction; and, as my spirituality waned, my indulgence in lust grew. This will happen no matter what the addiction.

The less we immerse ourselves in God and His ways, the more susceptible we are to the ways of the world which are never satisfying but always tempting. A happy Agnostic might disagree; but, if truly happy then a focus on love must be present; and this is the way of God. And, if the focus is only on loving and being loved by other people, then we are vulnerable to a crash of our happiness when we lose that love through either our choice or the choice of the other.

God's love of us is the only love that we can really count on to never die and will never be refused when sought. It is more perfect than human love though we usually don't differentiate. The *Bible* tells us that love is slow to anger but is referring to the love of man. The love of God, perfect love, Divine Love, knows no anger, no wrath. Anger is a creation of man we try to attribute to God; and it can become a self-destroying addiction. Indeed our prisons are filled with it; in fact, we may pronounce the same indictment for our society and our world. It works very cleverly with its partners of pride and greed which we also attempt to attribute to God at the same time we believe Him to be seeking their purging from us.

As we entered the eighties, our children were growing up, more moving of our home, more changes in my career, more restlessness in my heart as I grew further away from God and my family. Sure, I found plenty of excuses then; we always can, to justify our withdrawal, to justify our selfish actions. But the truth is, if we remain focused on Him instead of our problems, resting in Him, accepting the peace He offers, we can weather any storm. Yet we remain headstrong. We have to do it our way instead of His, while we can't even see what the truth is, while we're diverted from Him.

Fatal Attraction

Then the unthinkable happened in 1982. While I had been unfaithful to my wife hundreds, even thousands of times in my mind, I had never physically cheated on her, not once in our then twenty-one years of marriage. What can best be characterized as a fatal attraction took place. It certainly was fatal to my marriage as Pat and I divorced just days short of our twenty-third wedding anniversary. The ill-fated attraction was short lived, only a matter of weeks; yet, at the time, my vision was so corrupted, not only did I see it as true love to become marriage; but I saw it as a cure for my addiction instead of the reality of being a consequence.

Prior to our divorce in 1984, the full weight of what I had done came crashing down on me; and I saw I was losing everything in my life that really mattered. On a particularly hot

Central Florida day, with the sun at its height in the clear sky, I decided to run myself to the point of heat-stroke and death. You're right, really dumb! But remember, I wasn't thinking or seeing clearly at the time. I assure you, I was dead serious in my intended result. I had been used to running about three miles a day at the time; and, after about ten miles of frustration and anger at God for not allowing my plan to work, I returned home to find Pat angry and probably suspicious of where I had disappeared to. I felt like making another attempt but was too exhausted.

After the divorce, I started dating someone who had been a friend through my work; and we married before the end of the year of the divorce. It was a marriage that should have never happened for too many reasons to enumerate here, the main of which, of course, was my addiction. After a couple years, I ran away to Miami to what I told myself and my second wife was a career change and enhancement within the investment field.

Instant success in my new work quickly eroded into disaster. I became deeply depressed and again suicidal; but, before any attempt, discovered what was called a church with a different spin on salvation and life on earth. Though the doctrine was flawed, it helped me to face my problems instead of run from them. I soon quit what I determined was a pseudo-church. With no guarantees or financial assistance, I also quit the job I had run to as a fast track to riches and re-established my financial planning practice for a short time in South Florida.

Then, believing I could salvage the second marriage and control my addiction, I moved back to Central Florida. I was wrong on both counts. Soon divorce again reared its ugly head. In 1988, my youngest daughter became my workmate.

A Coping Addict

In spite of the addiction, two areas of my life were working fairly well: my work as a Certified Financial Planner and my working-out or physical fitness. When I ran away to South Florida, I had taken my son's old, rusted bicycle. I had been a runner for some time but had injured a knee on a tennis court so I replaced the running with swimming and cycling. Now, back in Central Florida, somewhat settled into bachelorhood, the focus on cycling increased, especially when I found a great buy on an Italian road bike. It seemed the swimming and the cycling had restored my knee while in Miami so I also returned to running.

This became the most disciplined, healthy part of my life; and I soon started participating in short-distance triathlons which became a passion. While younger athletes would pass me in the swimming and running phases, I would often zoom by them on the bicycle phase. This was a rush and fueled my competitive juices.

So, while I seemed to be doing pretty well with some aspects of my life, this didn't deter the downward spiral of the real me, my soul, which was becoming more bound by sexual lust. I might add that, all during my post-Cursillo era, I never abandoned God from a religious standpoint as I had remained a practicing Catholic. So I am both grateful to my church for that thread of connection and resentful because most organized churches do little to help in the area of addiction or habitual sin. Confession of my sin to a priest, at minimum, was useless and, at maximum, exacerbated the problem.

The Church

There is a tendency for churches to ignore addiction or, at best, allow their facilities to be used for secular methods of treatment. It would seem the general attitude is they are houses of worship and they must limit their activities to their ceremonies and preaching the *Bible*. Many seem to get involved in feeding the poor and homeless and visiting the physically sick and elderly, which is commendable; but they do little to free the bondage of addiction among their general congregations. They themselves are blind to the fact that their eloquent words can't reach the hearts of those lost souls who have "eyes that cannot see and ears that cannot hear."

They are blind to the fact that God isn't interested in their worship through ceremonies; but He is interested in love and what grows out of our love and, more important, His Divine Love. They delude themselves that they are magicians in changing bread and water into the substance of God; yet that substance does nothing to free the souls of the imprisoned members of the congregations. The *Bible* tells us the real substance of God, His Divine Love, will transform us into new creatures and it will; but this soul, "who was lost and now is found," who "was blind but now sees" with the eyes of Jesus, never found true freedom through a church.

Now the reader might here be tempted to say, "well if you had been a member of my church, you would have found freedom." Perhaps; but I see many churches and evangelists today appealing to emotions which may temporarily create a commitment to mend one's ways and turn to God's ways; but, as soon as we're back in the real world of day-to-day work and living and temptation, we lose our focus on God and redirect our focus on the world, which is family, work, debts, activities, things, etc. and we're too busy to stay focused on God all the time. It just isn't possible! Is it?

It's not only possible; but Jesus says its easy! He also tells us the solution comes not from without, the church, but from within, the soul, which may become the kingdom of God if we want it bad enough or better said, "good enough." Its time to stop buying the lies of the world and listen to the words of the one who every Christian says is his role model; but most don't follow. They say, "It's too hard, not enough time, not realistic in these times, not possible in my situation." Wrong! All lies fed to us by a world of greed and pride that wants to suck every drop of life from us. And all too often today, the church is a part of that life-sucking world; and some of the people running those false churches know it.

Jesus says its "easy;" and he doesn't lie. A church isn't necessary, never has been; but the church, which has nothing to do with buildings, which is you and me, committed children of God, committed to His way no matter what, is. These committed children see every person on earth as a precious child of God, no matter background, looks, or belief. And they believe it is their Father's will than none be lost and that His will will always be done.

Predestiny? Not quite. No hell? Yes hell, but not eternal.
More on these fascinating subjects later.

Incurable

Approaching age fifty, I happened on a TV talk show one
day where the single guest of attention was seated on a stage,
surrounded by a screen, revealing only his silhouette. Not being
in the habit of watching talk shows, this tweaked my curiosity.
Why didn't this man want his identity revealed? What was he
afraid of? As the dialogue between him and the host progressed,
I discovered the man was me. He was a sex addict. No, we
weren't identical in our manifestations; no two are; but we had
enough in common that I closely identified with this poor soul as
I do now with every addict, every criminal, whether jailed
behind concrete and wire and bars, or in mind only, as was this
talk show guest.

In addition to the subject guest, present were several so-
called experts, a psychologist who had been counseling the man,
and others with advanced degrees, denoting their expertise in the
working of the human mind.   Every one of the experts
pronounced our subject "incurable," that the best he could hope
for was to control his compulsions; but that the internal battle
would continue for the rest of his life, beyond the age when men
lose their sexual appetite, because the core of the affliction is
always other than simply an over-active libido.

In retrospect, I'm sure not a single one of these highly
educated people realized they were sentencing the man to life in
prison. Not a single one realized the damage they were capable
of perpetrating with such a pronouncement which, though
perhaps unintentional, was a lie. When we say anything is
incurable, we are recognizing the limitations of man and
ignoring the existence of an all-powerful Creator God who is
exhibiting those powers all around us all the time. In turn we
are exhibiting "eyes that cannot see and ears that cannot hear."

At the time of the talk show, this also pertained to me as I
bought the lies of the experts. And, since I identified with the
subject lost soul, I accepted that I too was "incurable." This in
spite of considering myself a Christian. But I had not been born

again and had not been transformed into a new creature as the *Bible* identifies a true believer, a true Christian, no longer living as Tom Lomas but as Christ living in and through Tom Lomas. Not yet!

I resolved that I would just have to live my life as well as I could; and that I would have to carry my plague to my grave. Perhaps then I would find relief. Sadly, this is not the case as those, who die as addicts, carry their addictions into the spirit world. There is no automatic transformation awaiting at death's door for those who simply intellectually believe in some premise put forth by their religions. We cannot become one with God in His habitat, one with Love, if we have not become love. Do we really believe Perfection will blend with imperfection? Then how can any enter His domain? For man this is impossible; but not for God if man allows; for the Almighty will never violate the free-will of His helpless child; and we are indeed all helpless, lost creatures without Him.

Maintaining the status-quo will not work with any addiction and did not with mine. As with Mr. Hyde and the good Dr. Jekyll, the addiction, the monster within, is never satisfied and must always have more. It is the same with any goal; when we reach the goal, whether it be family, business, sports, or anything other than God, somehow it isn't as satisfying as we thought it would be. After the initial euphoria, we may crash in depression if we don't rapidly set and work toward a new goal.

So many of us feel unworthy of God; yet the truth is He is the only goal worthy of us. It's the way He made us as our loving Father, to come home to Him, to live in friendship with Him, forever. As Jesus told us, He's waiting with open arms and the more soiled we are the more jubilant are the heavenly hosts when we invite Him into our hearts to give us His transforming Divine Love. As with the prodigal child, we can say, "Father I've blown it. I've bought all the lies of this world, chased all the false gods; and I'm still empty, still hungry; and now, at last, I know that hunger can only be satisfied by You. Come, my Father, fill me, satisfy my hunger that can only be satisfied by your Divine Love. Fill me, Father, fill me to overflowing with Your Divine Essence. Let me be one with You." This is the one prayer our heavenly Father will never refuse to grant if we pray it with true desire and soul-longing which are more important than the words.

Falling deeper into lust and more out of control, I no longer believed my psychiatrist from the sixties, who had said that I would never attack a woman. In my moments of guilt, I saw my complete loss of control was only a matter of brief time. I couldn't bear the thought of physically harming someone so I carefully planned a method for suicide that would not fail and that would appear accidental.

Surrender

Late one night, after a session with pornography and masturbation, on the brink of implementing my plan, I cried out one final desperate prayer to the God I still believed to be omnipresent. I called on what I had learned from nuns in first grade Christine Doctrine. "God, I can't live this way any longer. No one can help me, no one on earth, only you, Father. I believe You are all powerful. I believe, if You want to, You can heal me. Please, God, make it your will to heal me. Please!"

After this most emotional, most heart-felt prayer of my life, I was exhausted and fell into a deep sleep. When I awoke the next morning, the first thought that entered my mind was the answer to my prayer. I was jubilant! I knew I was about to be healed. The answer was just one short sentence, "You need to follow the example of Jesus' forty days in the desert." But with that brief answer was what I could only characterize as a huge download into my subconscious mind as I had no questions of the specific steps to implement what became my forty day journey in the desert of my soul.

II. THE DESERT

Truth

According to the *Bible*, after his baptism in the Jordan River by his cousin John called the Baptist and before starting his ministry, Jesus went into the desert by himself and fasted for forty days. Though the chronology of the New Testament is often challenged, I believe this narration to be properly placed from an historical standpoint. I believe his purpose was twofold, to draw closer to his Father and to confront his enemy. I believe he was motivated by the realization of both the importance of his mission and an awareness of his earthly end and how it was to come.

As far as we know, there were no mortal witnesses to this sojourn; therefore, if it really happened, we must assume he later told his apostles about it. More important than the reality of the story is its message which can also be said of much of the *Bible* and other great truths. Truth does not depend on history; it simply is.

If, indeed, Jesus did tell the story of his forty day battle against temptation in the wilderness, he must have had a reason. I would speculate the story does have a purpose as does everything that happens or is revealed to humankind. What do we learn from this story? Is it indeed possible that it concealed a message for almost two thousand years to be discovered by a man, not a theologian or *Bible* scholar, but a hopeless addict who was about to end his own life in lieu of hurting others? Is it possible that an all-loving God would reveal the meaning of this special message to one of His creation in desperate need? Are there other such concealed messages in the *Bible*, like the Parables of Jesus, which hold a special meaning for souls in desperate need?

Self Vs Oneness

If this is indeed so, then far more important than their historical truth is their truth in application of healing and salvation to the loved ones of God which we all, on this spaceship of earth, are. We are all brothers and sisters, everyone in the world, created not only for friendship with God but brotherhood with each other. Those who would foster separation and segregation are on the way out, the chauvinists, feminists, atheists, gay rightists, isolationists, Catholics, Protestants, and on, and on. These blessed souls think they seek freedom and justice but are out of harmony with their Creator when they foster separation. The doctrine Jesus taught was oneness with God and each other, losing self to gain eternity.

Equal rights cannot be legislated or forced by man; it is a gift from God that only needs to be accepted. As long as I know I have equal opportunity for an eternity in blissful union with my Father, why would I let those who strive for power or dominance in the world interfere with my peace, that great gift of the Father illuminated by Jesus? Indeed he told us, if we suffer in this regard, our reward will be great in heaven in contrast to those who seek assertion of self. If the Father accepts all who reach to Him, why would I spend my short time on earth reaching for less than Him and His Divine Love? We are here on this earth, as shown and taught by Jesus, not to fulfill self but to lose self and gain God.

Total Surrender

Unknown to me, God had been preparing me for the forty days in the desert of my soul for some time. My spiritual path began about age six with Christian Doctrine classes taught by nuns at my church. Religion has cluttered our picture of God; but the basics, all-powerful, all-present, all-wise, all-loving attributes, which were already known in my soul, were brought to my young conscious mind and stayed with me and were nourished by all the experiences of those first fifty years portrayed in Chapter One. It was a path which could be referred to as a spiritual lifeline or connection to God; and the nourishment came not only from the elevating experiences but also from the trials; for it was He who brought me through every one. He was there, with me, all along the way as He is with each of us, uniquely, as if each is His only child.

When I made that final desperate prayer on the brink of self destruction, I truly surrendered all. Certainly every addict who believes there is a God prays to be released from his prison; but it's a tongue-in-cheek prayer as with the story in the *Bible*   of the young, rich man who approached Jesus. He was addicted to wealth and indeed had made it his god; but it was an unsatisfying god. He knew there was something more. His love for money and the wealth of the world, though he had much, had left him empty. This is why he approached Jesus and asked what he should do.

We're led to believe he was a good man and had diligently kept the commandments, at least the ones Jesus enumerated to not commit adultery, not murder, not steal, not give false testimony, and to honor parents. Jesus' answer was to sell all he had and give to the poor thereby creating treasure in heaven and then follow the way of Jesus. But he couldn't let go of his wealth, his addiction. Though the addiction lied to him and didn't provide the satisfaction it promised, he couldn't let go. He was in prison and could not break free. He was afraid of losing his wealth, his security blanket, though he received no security, only emptiness and desire for something more. He refused to make a total surrender of the worthless god, which imprisoned him, to the only God who could free him.

So it is with the prayer of every addict. When he is asked to surrender all to be healed, he can't let go of the whole thing. Oh sure, he's willing to sacrifice the imprisonment, the compulsion. After love, freedom is perhaps the greatest natural desire of humankind. But there is usually some little piece of the addiction he just can't let go of, some part of the lie, often until he hits the bottom of his pit where he is facing his final choice, total surrender or death. Too many choose death. Oh, physically, they may seem alive but spiritually, inside, they're dead; and, usually, no matter what the addiction, their physical lifespans will be shortened. Too many also commit suicide, either directly through indulgence in the addiction, or through other means of ending their miserable lives, the author almost an example of the latter.

I had arrived at the point of my choice between momentary

death or surrender. And, even if I had not been able to muster the false courage or self-pity to do myself in, this was still truly a choice between life and death; and I chose life. I handed the whole ugly mess of my addiction to the God who had created me, surrendered all of it, no matter what that meant for my future. Whatever God would require of me would be worth the price to escape the hell of my making. My addiction had not only robbed me of my freedom but also my career and my greatest earthly treasure, my family.

Immersing in God

God responds to heartfelt prayer, to faith, to total surrender of the way of the world to His way. He will <u>always</u> respond to such prayer. And with His response, though brief, which has been my repeated experience, comes an avalanche of information. Though I did not hear a voice or experience an angelic manifestation or an instant transformation, I knew He had answered. Though I was very familiar with the scripture He sited and had heard it preached at mass many times over my fifty years as a Catholic Christian, this was new information that my mind and brain had never before received. Using the example of Jesus, I was actually going to experience my own sojourn of purging from worldly temptation in the desert of my soul, to confront my enemy face to face in mortal combat.

I knew I didn't need to stop eating food or isolate myself in some wilderness area. In fact, I didn't have to change any of my daily routine except for one thing, LUST! Sexual lust had to go, one day at a time. The method was pretty simple. Each day, at the beginning of the day, in solitude, I would immerse myself in the presence of God. This was done though a combination of reading, prayer, and meditation and would take no longer than a half hour; and most of that could be considered *Bible* study or study of other spiritual texts. Close to this time, I had been given a book entitled The Seven Story Mountain by Thomas Merton who rapidly became my favorite author and expanded my spirituality substantially beyond where it had grown through the Catholic Church and Cursillo.

Though I used the *Bible* somewhat, Merton's texts would

become my primary study source for knowledge of and closeness to God for the early years of my rebirth. I in fact would never have more than limited success with incorporating regular *Bible* study and would later discover this was not due to any mental deficiency on my part nor lack of desire to learn about God. Though I now see the *Bible* through different eyes than those I earlier used to study with clouded vision, lack of understanding, and blind faith as the only parameters of acceptance, I still regard it to be the Book of Life as it is filled with messages which show the path to overcoming obstacles between God and man and offers the keys to peace and joy both on earth and in eternity.

God of Wrath?

It was written that Jesus was tempted for forty days. I believe confronting his enemy was intentional on his part. In fulfilling his mission, he would not only be taking on the religious rulers as his adversaries but, also, the common people of his time as he attempted to show them not a God of wrath and retribution but a God of love who forgave their sins without the pointless sacrifices and ceremonies and rules imposed on them by their hypocritical, greedy rulers. His success was limited then with his own people as now with many who call themselves Christians who still see the god of wrath who could only be appeased for the sins of the generations, preceding Jesus and to follow, by the shedding of his son's blood. These believers are not believing in the truth that Jesus taught but rather in a blasphemy which impedes these followers of blind guides, and more impedes their guides or teachers, on their path to salvation.

Some would compare the sacrifice of God the Father to the intended sacrifice of Abraham in Genesis as an act of love and that Abraham believed that God would raise Isaac from the dead after his slaughter. However, the sacrifice of Isaac was stopped by a compassionate God. Paul supposedly wrote that God doesn't want sacrifices and that Jesus would be the last sacrifice. Eyes that cannot see refuse to see the contradiction in such a premise. Truly, would a God, who doesn't want sacrifices, want a last sacrifice?

Would a loving Father send his son to an agonizing, drawn-out, torturous death as an act of love for others that He will still condemn the majority to an eternal lake of fire? Would He perpetrate the crime against His son through the predestined sins of creatures He created out of love for the purpose of being His friends? Did this loving God change His mind about these Pharisees and Romans and the one Apostle, who betrayed Jesus, and decide they too should be sacrificed in eternity for the good of the select few who would indeed qualify to be His friends for eternity not by their good deeds but by their blind faith in a god of contradiction? Did He thus violate His own law of "you shall not kill" and His own law of not violating the free-will of man?

God of Love

The God of this believer loves every soul He created as if it was His only creation, loves every hair on the head of every human, and would not force any person to kill another; and, much less, would He through others kill His own son. This is the God who prevented my self-destruction as He will with all who choose to turn to Him. He is not the God of only the Christian though He is the One Jesus called Father. He is also the God of the Buddhist, the Hindu, the Moslem, the Western Indian, the Agnostic, the Atheist, etc. He is the God of all and His will is that none, not one, be lost; and, ultimately, none will; though many will endure much suffering through their own choice not His. This suffering pertains to not only those seen by the world as unrepentant criminals but also those who perpetuate, even when out of ignorance, false doctrines about our singular, all-loving God. God has created a universe of harmony; and man alone is the creator of disharmony. Only those in harmony with God and His immutable laws are permitted to enter His heavens where disharmony does not exist.

Forty Days

Also at the beginning of each of the forty days in the desert of my soul, I would mark the number of the day on a calendar. Some using the forty day procedure, as outlined in detail in my first book, mark the date of each day by the corresponding day number for each of the forty days in Chapter Six of *40 Days to Freedom* (www.40days2freedom.org). Since my first forty day journey, I have made many more for various purposes for purging other bad habits or to instill good habits or to simply draw closer to God. I have even made journeys as an intercessor for others and for physical ailments. I found, through experimentation with other record-keeping systems, using a separate monthly calendar, marking the number of each day, was most meaningful to me.

In the beginning I knew I must take each day one day at a time. I could not grasp the concept of going forty days without lusting; but I could grasp one day. Then marking each day separately, carefully, on my calendar was very special. Each day became a separate battle and, more important, a separate victory all its own and watching those victories accumulate was both encouraging and exhilarating. Each was a treasure that, somehow I knew, would last for an eternity. That, at this writing, was nine years ago. We have a long, glorious way to go, filled with wonderful journeys, loving every one and everyone involved with them.

When I received the simple answer to my prayer, I also received a vision where I was able to see my terrible adversary clearly for the first time. I was able to see that with my will-power, my strength, I never had a chance. Not the most powerful, willful, intelligent person in the world would have a chance to free himself from that adversary. I saw the absolute futility in my struggle against that mountain of deceit for almost forty years of my life. Yet, standing beside me, all that time, was an amply equipped knight in shining armor who was ready and willing to fight the battle for me. All I had to do was ask. And so I did: "All right, Lord, I get the picture! I surrender to your strength! You fight that monster for me!" And He did ..... one day at a time ..... each day a great victory ..... each day adding to a momentum of success ..... each day visibly recorded on my calendar.

Individual Vs Group Rehab

A Baptist Pastor, who uses *40 Days to Freedom* with groups

has devised a lesson plan, including journaling, for the entire God-given procedure contained in the book's one hundred sixty pages. The procedure includes six chapters of preparation for the journey, which is experienced in Chapter Six with each day having its own excerpt from Psalms, meditation, and prayer, and two post-experience chapters of what I think of as cementing and enlightenment. Both the lesson plan and *40 Days to Freedom* are available by contacting Freedom Ministries, Inc. through its web site (www.40days2freedom.org). The lesson plan was prepared for group involvement which, in my opinion, can either add to or subtract from the procedure.

In my desert experience, I was accountable to no one but God and myself. Since my journey was successful, that was certainly sufficient. From some who have experienced group involvement in overcoming, I have learned there can be a tendency for the individual to become dependent on the group. Dependence on God alone should be individually sought. Dependence on others not only makes us vulnerable to disillusionment through their imperfections but also puts an impossible burden on those on whom we depend whether they welcome our dependence or not.

That said, I do believe God has created each of us to be not alone. He wants us to serve each other and to allow Him to serve through us. In the latter we experience the easy yoke and light burden and the incomparable joy from allowing His love to flow through us to His other children, our brothers and sisters in Him. And, the greater the need for that love, the greater the joy and fulfillment in giving it. This is the whole meaning of Matthew 25.

So, I am saying, participate in group programs and group administration of *40 Days to Freedom*; but do so for the purpose of loving and being loved by God through others. Do not attempt to possess the group nor any in the group and do not allow the group to possess you lest it too becomes an addiction. And, when taking the forty day journey in the desert of your soul, do so apart from other humans as Jesus, our role model, did. And, as with our role model, use only the strength of the

Father and none of your own or others. A prison minister of twenty five years, while sharing about *40 Days to Freedom* by phone, once expressed to me, "Tom, if even Jesus, the son of God, had to use his Father's strength to overcome the enemy, what chance do we have if we don't?"

Strength of God

All well and good; but how do you do that? How does one use only the strength of the Father? Again, we look to our role model. From both the historical and Biblical evidence about Jesus, we know His focus was constantly on God. He taught, contrary to the religions of his time, of a God of love. And not only did he teach it but he practiced it; he virtually exuded love to the ultimate expression of unselfish, agape love in giving his own life, both in the living and in the dying, that others might be free. Indeed, this author sees him as love incarnate. In addition, are the many references of his prayerfullness, sometimes to the extent he would spend the entire night in prayer to the Father.

Not much is revealed about his study; but we can assume that he steadily progressed in His knowledge of the Father, both prior to and during his ministry, as he exhibited a competence in his knowledge and faith, probably greater than any had before him or since. I believe his sources were the ancient scriptures and his *Internal Bible* and angels and the spirit of the Father Himself, all the same sources available to every one of us. And, like Jesus, if we immerse ourselves in the Father, we can saturate ourselves with His strength and defeat any temptation or compulsion. This is what he meant when he told us we would not be tempted beyond our endurance.

The world's way says, "Work out your own problems; and, if you're weak, rely on the group, reinforcing each other. You will learn to overcome your compulsions, though the battle against them must continue; and you must truthfully claim always to be an addict." God's way says, "Do not resist evil; rather, focus on Me. I will take all your burdens and make them easy and light, one day at a time. And I will set you totally free and give you the eyes of Jesus that you may see Me in truth. You are my precious child for whom I desire only the best on earth and in heaven." I did; and He did!

The same routine was employed every day; and, instead of immersing myself in lust at the local health club at the beginning of each day, as I heretofore had, I immersed myself in Father God. Now this is important. I <u>did not</u> avoid temptation. I still worked out at the health club. Jesus did not avoid temptation in either his desert experience or his ministry. Indeed, he told us he came to call sinners which meant, as the *Bible* portrayed, he mingled with them. And his greatest temptation, of which he demonstrated precognizance, though greatly troubled and, no doubt, tempted to escape, as the final hour before his arrest approached, he faced squarely and defeated as he commended his spirit into his Father's hands.

WWJD?

We all have to face our crosses, our burdens every day. Do we face them squarely using a power we are promised will always overcome? Or do we struggle in misery making the burden heavier than it is? Or do we escape to our addictions which, rather than solving our problems, exacerbate them? WWJD? It appears too simple to our human intellect which loves to complicate. So it was in Jesus' day with the religious rulers. So it is today again with the religious rulers and the psychologists. "What would Jesus do?" is not the question; it is the answer to all our questions. He did not resist evil or problems. He did nothing on his own, even the words he gave us he told us were from the Father.

WWJD? He focused on the Father, gave it to the Father, surrendered to the Father's strength, was one with the Father, as we all may be. He allowed the Father's strength, the Father's Divine Love, to work through him, to flow through him. This is what he meant when he told the Apostles in seeing him they were seeing the Father. Thus his yoke was easy and burden light. Thus he loved his life; he loved his work; he loved <u>all</u> people, even the infamous Pharisees and Scribes; and, above all, he loved his Father who is Divine Love. Of all the attributes of God this Divine Love is the main, the ruling one; and there are none in Him which are contrary to it, not anger, not wrath, not condemning judgment, not unforgiveness, not destruction of any of His creation which is all brought to being in His awesome love.

Fasting

So none of my daily routine changed except for the addition of taking on the strength of the Father and, of course, my fast. My addiction was my fast though I truly never thought of it in that way until years later, when sharing with inmates at the Orange County Jail, I was asked if I had gone without food for my forty days. Before I was able to answer that this was not God's direction to me, another inmate responded, "His addiction was his fast." I was immediately humbled and, for a moment, speechless as I realized and then expressed to the others that we had just been given Divine Revelation through this "brother in blue" (a common reference among prison ministers and inmates).

At the time of this writing, fasting against food for forty days is becoming more popular with many Chistian movements throughout our country; and, though I have never participated beyond the ritual fasts and abstinence of Catholics, I accept that this Biblical ritual may be a way for healthy people to draw closer to God as He gives us a plethora of means for this. By healthy, I mean healthy in body and soul. I also feel it is a mistake for anyone, who is bound by addiction or habitual sin, to go without food for forty days if they are not also fasting against their sin.

I can further state that, had I attempted to go without food in my first desert experience, the additional burden would have worked against me and certainly was not necessary as the results of a complete lifting of my affliction testifies. Again, my Divine direction had nothing to do with food; though, indeed, the scriptures state that Jesus went without food. We also have reason to believe, again based on scripture, that he was indeed healthy in body and soul.

The question may come to mind, what if the addiction is food? By personal observation, I have not witnessed overweight people, who participate in forty day food fasts, who thus become slim. To my surprise, they tend to remain overweight. Though not an addiction, I have, in my younger adult years had a problem with overeating and overweight though not extreme. I overcame the problem through changing the foods I was eating, while maintaining a healthy exercise regimen, and the weight dropped off. This while I was in my lust addiction.

Replacing Addiction with God

Two important points here. First, in "The Guide to Live the Miracle" of *40 Days to Freedom*, I recommend that with food addiction one seek professional help in establishing a healthy eating regimen and then stick to it, using our forty day procedure, again, relying not on one's own strength but only on the strength of Father God. I believe most nutrition professionals would also encourage exercise to be combined with diet. But the key here is not the rote repetition but the spiritual ingredient. Thus you are establishing the healthiest habit in the universe along with eliminating a bad one. You are learning to "Tap the Greatest Power" (Chapter Eight of *40 Days to Freedom*) on a daily and more frequent basis. For this reason, I prefer to not refer to the forty day procedure of our books as a fast which infers sacrifice because the most important part is receiving through spiritual rebirth.

The second important point is to use the forty day procedure the first time to defeat the greatest enemy, the one which imprisons us, the worst habitual sin or addiction or obsession. This may be hidden from our conscious minds; therefore prayerful analysis is necessary. As earlier stated, I had a tendency to blame anything but the addiction for my problems; and, though I felt I was a monster, I was not aware of the degree of my enslavement. Further, the overcoming of my poor eating habits had no affect on my lust addiction. This may be contrary to the advice of some professionals; but it is the absolute truth as experienced by this healed addict.

In addition, we are aware of some so-called professionals recommending the substitution of one, a lesser addiction, for one more powerful or destructive. This is a deadly course of action with one exception: substituting an addiction to God and His loving way. Often when speaking before groups, I refer to God as the only healthy addiction; but, in truth, this is inaccurate as He never enslaves as an addiction. He <u>always</u> sets free.

This is why it takes conscious effort on our part to stay connected to Him. Otherwise, if He would become a human addiction we would not be His friends which the *Bible* tells us He created us to be. Friendship denotes free choice, both ways. No one can be forced to be another's friend.

No Perfect Religion

We feel the need to make the necessary distinction here that religion and its man-created and imposed dogmas can, and often does, become addiction. The cure is the same as for other addictions or obsessions as we have herein proposed and experienced. Indeed my Catholicism was a form of addiction. I still regard myself as a Catholic, a contemplative, born-again Catholic, who views all religions with the discerning eyes of Jesus, now understanding that no religion has all of the truth while all have some. At the same time I appreciate the plight of members of all religions, who are endeavoring to believe the teachings of their leaders.

If, indeed, Christianity, or one of its many denominations, was the perfect religion, why is it the most splintered and divided of all the major religions of the world? Why do Christians war against and even kill other Christians? The answer is God's refusal to interfere with man's free-will which man has used to twist and alter God's direction. God will not violate this immutable law, even in the writing of scripture, even in the writing of *40 Days to Freedom*, even in the writing of *The Man in the Desert*. We are, however, aware of a more accurate means for conveying the Word of God and one perfect means. Both will be defined in this book.

The Core Addiction

I network with recovery professionals and ministers throughout the world. At a recent meeting at a recovery camp in South Florida, the observation was made that many, who participate in an eight month, Christ-centered, drying out from substance abuse program, shortly after reentering the world, fall again to their substance abuse because upon reentry they first fall to illicit sex which was the core addiction. Amazingly, after the observation was expressed, not by this author, seeming little or nothing was done to correct the problem with the curriculum.

It would seem that, while our society readily recognizes some behaviors as addiction, others, which may be the deeper obsession, are ignored to the detriment of all involved, especially the addict, who, when able and free from isolation, will again succumb to the untreated core compulsion. Indeed today, it would seem, our entire society, even many so-called religious, accept what Jesus defined as illicit sex as the norm and thus a single addiction wearing many faces can corrupt an entire country to the point that its dreadful acts, even by the leader of a nation, can be condoned by a majority of the populous or, if not condoned, at least looking the other way at what they perceive as more important issues.

There is no more important issue than the Godlessness of a nation, founded as a nation under God, which has come to the point of having eyes which cannot see and ears which cannot hear, which has made money and materialism and sex and violence its gods. Such a nation doesn't need a forty day fast against food but against immorality, along with a forty day focus on God through study, prayer, and meditation. And we are not referring only to the God of the Christians, who often see Him less clearly than others, but the God who is the One loving Creator Father of us all.

Strength in Weakness

Though I claim no revelation in the matter of Jesus' forty days in the desert, I believe his fasting against food may have been to intentionally lower his resistance and ability to use his own strength against temptation along with increasing his focus on the Father. I believe, by this time in his life, he had knowledge of what lay before him, including the ultimate penalty he would have to pay for teaching the truth, which struck at the heart of the religious tradition of his day. And, because of that penalty, not only would he be tempted to escape or deny his God-given truth; but he would also be tempted to soften his message and avoid angering his adversaries to the point of his execution on the cross.

Thus, in a way, by weakening himself, he was tempting his spiritual adversaries to do battle with him and, by using only the strength of his Father in quoting scripture, the accepted word of God, to his adversary, he proved what Paul later stated as, "When I am weak, then am I strong;" and he showed us the way, or rather that his example is the way, to fight all our temptations, not by avoiding them, not by resisting them, but by facing them squarely and using only the strength of the Father. Indeed, He will face all our problems, fight all our battles, if we will only let Him.

I have been inspired to add here a noteworthy aspect of the desert story of Jesus. His adversary also quoted scripture to Jesus as a part of his tempting. Rather than take the bait and respond, "No, devil, you're improperly using that scripture; you are attempting to apply literally that which my Father intended for different application," he simply properly applied another scripture thereby choosing to <u>ignore the evil</u> and <u>focus on the good</u>.

Likewise, today, there are fanatics with their own agenda of judgmentalism who will misapply words from the *Bible* to prove not what is inspired by God but by their own religious addiction. These are people who are feigning happiness and peace and fulfillment at the direction of their religious leaders who tell them Christians are supposed to be happy and set an example that attracts others, which is true; but, if it has to be forced or faked, something is very wrong with the Christianity thus professed. In fact, most who claim to be Christians are not truly happy and free from worry, are not content with their lives, are frustrated, are feeling that something is missing; and they are right. They are following a false Christianity and a false use of the *Bible* and are reaping their just rewards.

Revelation is Continuous

This was not the intent of our Father with His Divine Revelation, which is in the *Bible*; but which has been severely altered by man. This was not the purpose for which He sent

Jesus; but again man has severely altered that blessed purpose. When we are told that nothing should be added to or taken away from the *Bible* this doesn't mean, as man misinterprets, that God's instruction to man stopped sixteen hundred years ago. It means that we should not twist or change His revelation to our own purpose. Thank God, His revelation is continuous; otherwise we would have little chance for discerning the truth in the garbled mess created by man.

As I share with you the truth I have learned in my sixty years on this earth, I have no aspirations as to the success or failure of this work. This was true with *40 Days to Freedom*; and the same is true here. I had no knowledge that I would write another book and considered the continuing printing and free distribution of 40 Days to be a full-time job for the rest of my life; and well it could have been, except for God's direction which has been with the second, as with the first, a continuous grooming and preparation for His purpose revealed in His time. As with 40 Days, though I began this writing two months ago, I have been writing this book all my life. No aspirations, just obedience. This makes my life today very simple and peaceful and fulfilling to just obey my Father and leave any results to Him.

Experience the Power

Each day of my first 40 day journey, was an immersing in the greatest power in the universe, through study, meditation, and prayer, absorbing it like a sponge. Each day resolving to just say "NO," through this power, for just this one day, against my greatest sin, the sin which most separated me from God, the sin which had stolen my freedom and imprisoned me. Each day marking my calendar simply with the number of the day of my journey in the desert of my soul, watching the days of victory, through God's strength alone, accumulate behind me. Each day, while marking that number, feeling the elation of knowing I was one day closer to a freedom I had never before known.

Again, in *40 Days to Freedom* the last chapter of spiritual instruction is titled "Tap the Greatest Power." The participant truly starts doing just that when he first picks up the book and reads the cover. He will experience God's power intensifying within him as he progresses through the chapters of preparation for his journey in the desert of his soul. Through this accumulating and growing power, he will learn more not only of the Divine Power he reaches for, God the Father, but also of the man who used that power to human perfection, Jesus of Nazareth, and the man or woman who is about to follow in the footsteps of the Nazarene.

But just exactly what is this power we are attributing to the Creator of the universe as the Source? In a word, LOVE, not the puny love of man but the transforming Divine Love of God. Relating to the knight of my vision, I thought of faith as my shield and love as my weapon against my enemy, my addiction, my personal demon.

There was an ebb and flow to this first and all-important journey. On some days I would experience struggle and the need for more immersing in the Power. On other days my spirit would seem to soar to the extent that no enemy could touch me.

Born Again!

Then, around Day 20, there was a great change. Suddenly, I was aware that everything was somehow different. Everywhere I looked I saw beauty, God's beauty, in everything, in His creation, in man's creation, and especially in the eyes of other people. No matter what they looked like, no matter what they had done, I could see how much each person was loved by the Creator of us all. It was as if I was viewing the world through different eyes. I thought, "This must be the way Jesus saw the world, through eyes of love which saw the beauty and glory of the Father everywhere." From that moment on, my circumstances on this earth became less important and my relationship with God more important.

At the time, I didn't have a full understanding of what had happened, but thanks to the inspired word of God, the subject of spiritual rebirth was amazingly well explained in the book which gave the procedure to the world. This life-changing experience of being born again, which Jesus defined as the only means to attain the celestial home of his Father, is the greatest evidence of

41

the truth of his teaching and the existence of an all-powerful, all-loving, Creator God. Nothing else, aside from man, in all of His creation has received this gift, this potential for rebirth and complete transformation into a new creature. And as with the addict, only one who has walked in the shoes of the reborn can understand its power and impact.

This is what transformed eleven close associates of Jesus from cowards in hiding, after his physical death, into the forming pillars of Christendom, after his resurrection; and all but one bravely giving their lives in martyrdom, as did Jesus, their leader, for the truth he taught and gave to the world. And so it has been with many that have been added to his flock right down to the present time with this year the slaying of students at Columbine High School who gave their lives rather than deny their God as well as the many throughout the world in places where religious freedom is unknown. This is indeed the greatest gift any can give for it will inspire many to seek the rebirth through which individual human beings become one with God, receiving His very essence in their souls, never to be replaced by any invader and transforming the receiver truly into a new creature of God.

This is the way to the Father through the son of which Jesus taught and gave his life that we might receive eternal life in celestial bliss. But it is bestowed only on those who seek to receive this Divine Love of the Father who, of their own free-will, seek true oneness with Him. And, to those who seek it sincerely, with all their hearts and all their souls and all their minds and all their strength, it is never refused, regardless of denomination, regardless of religion.

This is not an exclusive gift, as some teach, only for those who call themselves Christians but is inclusive of all of God's children which we all on the face of this earth are. Further, it is not an automatic gift as some profess which comes through a statement of faith in Jesus. Rather, it is given, as Jesus taught, only to those who earnestly seek it, not with their minds or intellect but with the very hearts of their souls. This is what he meant when he taught the only way to the Father was through

42

him, not through the man, or through professing him God, or the equal of God, which he told us he was not, but through his teaching, the message of rebirth he was sent to give.

Free at Last!

Around Day 30 of my desert sojourn, I became aware my compulsion was gone and knew it was gone for good, never to return. I was reminded of "whom the son sets free is free indeed." In the many years since this healing, I have been sexually tempted many times but have not fallen once, not in mind, not in body, not in soul. And, as with my role model, I have not isolated myself from temptation. I am in the world, around sexy women every day; yet my yoke is easy and my burden light.

I claim no credit for this but give all credit to Father God through whose strength He fulfilled the promise He gave through Jesus that we won't be tempted beyond our endurance. I believe Jesus' entire life was a model of this; and, now, I no longer believe; but I know through my own experience. Whenever I fall in any way, it is only because I don't use the Father's strength. And, if we don't constantly immerse ourselves in it, we will fall, even if we're born again. There is no middle ground, only the way of the world or the way of God. If we don't make a choice, we choose the way of the world which is always, diligently, "like a roaring lion," pursuing us to enslave us.

I can still be physically attracted to a woman; but I don't compulsively undress her and more in my mind. I see her first as a beautiful creation of the same God who created me. I have no desire to abuse her or, for that matter, any of God's creation. She is my sister, no matter what she wears, how she looks, or what she believes. Above all, I love her with the love of Jesus, the love he literally died to give through teaching and living the message from his Father.

Now, Jesus did make the ultimate sacrifice; and we will devote an entire chapter to it; but the purpose for his life was not his death. The purpose for his life was the TRUTH he taught about the rebirth and that we all can be one with his Father and

43

our Father, his God and our God. Perhaps, if the Christian teachers of today would correct this misfocus on his tragic brutal death and instead recognize this as his exclamation of the truth he taught during his life, his very fulfillment of those truths of loving enemy and not resisting evil and drawing all strength from the Father and the triumph of good over evil and the reward for those who suffer and sacrifice that others may be free, perhaps the world would become less violent, less selfish.

And the sacrifice of which we speak is not one to appease an angry god, not to take on oneself the sins of another which is an impossible concoction of man characterized by the scapegoat of the Old Testament. The God of Jesus will have no part in the destruction of any of His beloved creation. The sacrifice of which we speak is an emptying of oneself, of giving one's all, even earthly life if need be, for the only worthwhile purpose for such sacrifice, to set others free from untruth.

It is the TRUTH he taught which sets us free not his death. Yet, if he had not paid the ultimate price on the cross, his Father's truth would have had to wait for a future generation. Not a word of the truth he gave would have been written; for, by saving his own life, he would have denied the very truth he taught. He did not take our sins. We reap what we sow. We are each individually accountable for our own sins and for the sins of our communities and those of our nation. The only exception to each of us paying every penny of this debt, either here on earth or in eternity or both, is the washing, the transforming power, of receiving the Divine Love of God through the New Birth.

Though I knew I was totally and irrevocably healed before the end of forty days, I continued, as each day before the healing, to the completion of the forty. This is what my role model had demonstrated; and I would not short his lesson. Also, I thought of the additional days as a cementing of the process.

But the last ten days were different. Before I had looked at each day as an individual victory that I knew would culminate in my healing. Now, I was healed! The victory was complete! I had won, or rather, God, my champion, my knight in shining armor, had won for me against impossible odds. I say impossible because not only had I been in this addiction for almost forty years, and been classified by society and science as "classic neurosis," "masterful instinct," "incurable;" but I had lost all hope of recovery. Not even religion and prayer had helped.

Surrender to God

Yet, the key to receiving the answer to that final desperate prayer was very simply SURRENDER, an attitude that said, "I have failed, Father; nothing I have tried has worked; I have no answers; I am at last willing to totally let go of the whole thing, to sacrifice anything and everything You require; do with me what You will; only please, please heal me." And He did.

God can't work with a selfish agenda. He knows that self is death to spirit. Jesus told us who loves his life will lose it; but who loses his life for the love of others will gain eternal life. This doesn't mean we should all become martyrs; but that we should give of ourselves to others, while living, on a daily basis, and not just to our families but to the others who are tough to love such as the homeless, the prisoners, and, yes, even our enemies. Jesus told us simply loving our family members and those easy-to-love people is nothing special. Indeed, we can do that on our way to hell.

It's not that God doesn't love us when we're selfish. He loves all equally, at all times, and has counted every hair on every head. He broke the mold for each one of us. But, when we are selfish, we ourselves block the lines of communication with our Father. We are going against the last and greatest commandment of the Father, given by Jesus, to love one another as he loved us. This is selfless or agape love which opens our lines of communication and our path back to Him.

Now some would respond, "That doesn't sound like any fun;" but, they are seeing with eyes that cannot see and hearing with ears that cannot hear. Further, if they tried it, they would like it. In fact, not only would they like it; but they would find a new way of living that would give a solution to the emptiness they experience from a constant quest for fun or self-satisfaction which can never be satisfying and is always disappointing. The law of sowing and reaping also pertains to giving; and, if we give love, become a conduit of His love, and leave the reaping to God, He will fill us to overflowing with His gifts which can even include the material if in accord with His purpose.

Can you imagine the joy I experienced in those last ten days? I had been blind, even while religious, all my life. Now, at age fifty, I could see with the eyes of Jesus. I had been lost, as the prodigal son, in the desert of false promises of the world. Now, I was found and welcomed home by my all-loving, all-forgiving Father. He entered my soul, at my invitation, through his Holy Spirit, to take permanent residence and transform this wayward life into a new creature with a new beginning of a new life destined to grow in blissful oneness with Him for eternity. Finally, I had been freed from the personal demon that had enslaved and chained my life to a horrible sin against my fellow humans and separated me from the God I desired to know. My joy was and has remained uncontainable This is why I must write this book, not only because God has so ordained, but also because my joy is uncontainable, must spill over, must be shared.

Perfection

Also, this is a story that must be told, at any risk, because the need is so great. I have with my own ears heard pastors estimate that two-thirds of their church members are not living Christian lives, are in bondage to the world. If the Christianity of the organized churches is the only true religion, how is this possible? I believe the members of the congregations are not only seduced by the world but also, in this information age, see their religion filled with contradictions and not to be taken seriously. Indeed, they also see that even their religious leaders seem unable to model the humble life of Jesus. A recent survey of pastors found one third admitting to sexual impropriety as pastors.

"They are only human," you respond. This is a favorite cliché used today to justify almost anything. If it has any truth, then why did Jesus tell us to be perfect as our Heavenly Father is

46

perfect? This we pass off as unrealistic, especially in our complicated world of business and science and technology and lawsuits of today. And it truly is unrealistic for man to be perfect or happy or fulfilled or peaceful today through his own strength, his own natural love, which has evolved since his first disobedience to his Creator to the lustful, prideful, greedy, angry love of man today.

Correct! Man is only human and cannot be perfect .... on his own! But he can be perfect, not in the eyes of man, but in the eyes of God, if <u>he</u> allows <u>God</u> to live in and through him! This is the only way, the way, the truth, and the life, given to us by the model of the perfect man, Jesus the Christ. It is the way, the truth, and the life we are <u>all</u> created to be. And, perfect, man must become, if he desires to become a resident of the highest Celestial Heavens; for Perfection will not become one with imperfection.

Do not dispair! Humankind has more help and more time allotted than is granted in this mortal, earthly coil. And we are reminded by our role model, "with God all things are possible." All He asks of us is the sincere desire and longing of our hearts for oneness with Him. His response will <u>always</u> be to send His Holy Spirit to fill us with His transforming Divine Love, giving us the eyes of Jesus, and marking us for eternal residence in His Celestial Kingdom.

III. The Eyes of Jesus

Destiny

There is a destiny, a Divine Purpose, for the existence of each one of us. None is forced to accept it. Jesus of Nazareth found his or, better said, surrendered to his, the will of his Father, which he identified as having come to call sinners and free the captives. The cross was not his purpose, was not the will of his Father. What earthly father would send his son, especially the son defined as the "only begotten son," to such an horrendous earthly ending? Is this the God of love exhibiting a lesser love than that of man? Or would we believe the God of creation loved mankind more than His son and thereby justified the sacrifice? If God is no respecter of persons, plays no favoritism as the *Bible* declares, and, indeed, as I believe, is one of His immutable laws, belief in this sacrifice from a God, who, again, the *Bible* tells us doesn't want blood sacrifice for removal of sin, will not enhance anyone's path to oneness with Him.

Truth

The purpose for this alteration or manipulation of God's purpose by man was simply to preserve tradition adopted by the Jews from still more ancient traditions. All of Jesus' initial apostles were Jews, as were most of their followers, so this was a natural carry-over. The intention, no matter how noble or innocent in its origin or continuance, does not justify the act of such manipulation. This is a classic example of man trying to remake God in his image. The time has come to correct this error. The concept that, somehow, every word written in the *Bible* by men is infallible is false and not promulgated by God. We can accept divine inspiration; but, when flowing through fallible, human instruments, some error is bound to occur.

I make every effort to implore the Almighty Father that the message He transmits through me be as pure and direct from him as possible; but even this enlightened work cannot be totally free from error. I believe it to be more free, though a larger work than my first, *40 Days to Freedom*, which has a more orthodox perspective. This doesn't mean one is a lie and the other the truth. In each case I have disclosed the truth as I have grown in its knowledge through the revelation of God, both direct and indirect though others. Indeed, my two works of a different time show a parallel progression as from the Old Testament to the New Testament. The progression doesn't mean the old no longer has value but may indicate, in each case, the earlier and later works were written for different people in different times or circumstances. And, for some, the two works can work together. I continue to take forty day journeys using my original text and often marvel at its harmony with the more recent revelation shared in this newer work.

So, as I believe most *Bible* scholars and theologians would agree, we must take the work as a whole to see the picture it presents; and we need to look for the special message within each story of the *Bible* instead of hanging on every word as historical fact. The truth is in the message conveyed to each reader for his unique application; but never should we accept a message from any source portraying our Father Creator as being anything contrary to the God of love whose very essence is Divine Love.

This does not mean we must fear eternal damnation if we contradict a false doctrine derived from the *Bible* as, indeed, Jesus, according to the *Bible*, corrected the premise to hate one's enemy, attributed to Moses. Jesus also exhibited displeasure with the law giver's condoning of divorce. A friend once commented to me he believed God intentionally allowed the existence of human error in the *Bible* as a challenge to the discernment of man, what I think of as the use of our *Internal Bible*.

Therefore, when we hear or read something in the *Bible* that feels uncomfortable with our soul, not our intellect, we should pay attention. Also, if we have not been born again, we cannot clearly see or hear the truth. Our connection to our *Internal Bible* is blocked; and that blockage may vary anywhere from complete spiritual dormancy, if we completely ignore God and the spiritual tools He makes available to us, to a flicker of a light if we blindly follow our religious leaders without seeking growth on our own. Rebirth gives us the eyes of Jesus which allow us to better connect to our *Internal Bible*, our knowledge of God, stemming from the creation of our souls.

Immortality

It is not uncommon for us to experience some discomfort along with the peace and joy of our rebirth. The peace and joy come from an awareness, not necessarily given words, from our *Internal Bible* that we are now immortal and destined for a growing, eternal oneness with the Lord of the universe. The discomfort comes from knowing something is amiss with our religion. This is a reason why we will often see people switch churches or denominations after their spiritual awakening. We might not know exactly what is wrong; but we are suddenly aware our present affiliation is not the total truth so we begin to search and sometimes in the wrong places.

Imperfection

I have been sorely tempted to leave the Catholic Church as God has revealed more of His truth to me. But, He has also shown me that no denomination; and, indeed, no religion has all the truth; but all have some of the truth; and some is better than none though we each should continue to strive and grow in His daily revelation to each of us individually. He has shown me leaving one imperfect church for another imperfect church makes little sense. Jesus was a Jew and was aware of the imperfections of his religion; yet, he worked for change and enlightenment among his people. He even had limited success with some of the religious leaders of his time. Perhaps we can hope a few, of what should be a more enlightened generation, will see the truth in this work.

New Birth

Jesus came to open the gates of heaven as the first of many divine sons and daughters of the living God. He did this by bringing the message of the New Birth through which man receives the Divine Love of God into his soul and begins a new life that leads to his final transformation as he enters the Celestial Abode of the Most High. The evidence we are given of this New Birth occurring in each one of us is the most powerful testimony of transformation which can be witnessed by man, what I have referred to as the eyes of Jesus. This was the only definition I could give to what happened in the middle of my first forty day journey in the desert of my soul.

About a month after completion of that first of many forty day journeys, I was basking in my newly discovered "heaven on earth." With my new eyes and reborn soul, life and its challenges took on a whole new perspective. My day-to-day problems didn't vanish. In some respects they increased in number; but they also lessened in intensity, that is the intensity of their impact on my feeling of well-being. Realizing I was a loved child of my Father God, with an eternal future of bliss ahead of me, my earthly problems were becoming not obstacles to my increased faith but, to the contrary, as with Jesus, stepping stones in the growth of my surrender to God and His perfect will, His plan for me.

God's Direction

A persistent thought, that I should write a book about this forty day procedure, entered my mind. I immediately dispelled this as I had proven that I could never be an author. In the seventies, with the apostolic zeal imbued in my life by the Cursillo experience, I had on two occasions attempted spiritual writing. In each case, after a short burst of enthusiastic composition, I would seemingly run out of words; and my inspiration would wane; and the project would be forgotten. So I would repeatedly reject this new notion without giving any consideration to its possible origin.

After about two weeks of this persistent intrusion, early one morning, while getting dressed for work, I heard a voice powerfully speak four words. Now, to my knowledge, my pet cat , Ucf, and I were the only occupants of my one-bedroom condo; and, usually, Ucf didn't have much to say, only an occasional "meow" when his food dish was empty. So I was momentarily startled until I realized the content of the message and its overpowering meaning. The words were "this is the reason;" and I knew God was telling me the reason for everything I had experienced in my life, to that point, had happened, or was allowed to happen, was to prepare me to write the book that would be His instrument of freedom from bondage to addiction and habitual sin.

I was also aware that this was the reason He had used a procedure to free me rather than an instant lifting of the compulsion which, to my knowledge at that time, was His more common approach, usually thought of as miraculous healing. Others would relate to a procedure far easier than an instant healing. This has been our experience with the abundance of fruit we have seen through *40 Days to Freedom*. And it is pure procedure, no biography as differentiated from this work.

Strangely, when I received the message which orchestrated my healing, there was no question, "Why am I given a forty day procedure when others receive instant healing?" I was too overjoyed with the answer from God and the knowledge that my forty year plague was soon to be lifted if I followed instructions. I still had the choice to accept or reject, to claim freedom through this extraordinary message or to doubt, to act or do nothing.

So it is with all the Father's direction, no forcing, more like gentle persuasion. Even while I stubbornly refused to receive the message to write 40 Days, He patiently persisted until He was able to really get my attention. Even then, I still had the ability to reject the offer. But how could I refuse? He had freed me from my lifetime imprisonment of my own creating. Gentle persuasion but, at the same time, powerful. His will was done as, even now, His message of freedom is blanketing the earth through 40 Days. And the blanketing and the freedom will become more widespread with the addition of *The Man in the Desert*.

Rebirth and Healing
As stated, rebirth and healing from God may be instantaneous or gradual. A prison minister brother was healed from drug addiction overnight. My path to rebirth started with a stirring in my soul on a weekend retreat in my early twenties. It was enhanced with what I think of as a great spiritual

awakening, when I discovered the humanity of Jesus, during my Cursillo experience in my early thirties. But what I think of as my moment of rebirth happened during that first forty day journey at age fifty. Even then, I wasn't able to pinpoint the exact day or hour. I simply became aware that my vision had changed and I was seeing everything and everyone differently, around the twentieth day, without knowing exactly when it had happened.

Likewise, about ten days later, I was suddenly aware that my lustful compulsion was gone with the knowledge that it was gone for good, never to return. Again, I was unable to pinpoint the exact moment of lifting or healing. It was as if God had snuck up on me, quietly worked a change, and vanished without my being aware of His work until after the fact..

I have a similar experience with contemplative prayer, when around eight minutes into prayer, I become suddenly aware, visually, of God's presence without knowing the exact moment. I believe this element of surprise is intentional on God's part. I believe this goes hand-in-hand with His sense of humor.

Uh-oh, what's this? Am I remaking God in the image of man? No, I am simply speaking of my personal encounters with Him. For example, I often experience His revelation and direction through what I think of as puzzles where He gives me one piece at a time. Ultimately, there is a key piece that brings all the rest together accompanied by a rush of elation. An example would be this book.

Revelation by Puzzle

I had no revelation that I was to author a second book until early one morning in May, 1999, when I observed a very small picture on the back of a book I was reading, the title of this work jumped into my mind; and, with that title, all the pieces that had been given over the last three years came flying together as if in a great rush; and I did experience a great rush of revelation and emotion and the intense awareness of the presence of the Father's Spirit.

I believe God not only observed all this but that He delighted in it. As if He exclaimed, "He got the picture!" "The message got through!" I believe He rejoices every time His message gets through to the understanding of any one of us, His blessed children.

So often we're like the rebellious teenager who doesn't listen. Then, when we finally do, our Parent is pleased. I can think of no more worthy goal for humanity than to bring a smile to our Father's experience every day. Unfortunately, I believe far too often, He experiences pity through our insistence of our way over His.

The Three Temptations

Through the ages, God has repeatedly offered His freedom to man by giving him free-will, the ability to reason and make choices. In the story of Adam and Eve we can see that man can be deceived or tempted by the world and the pleasures it offers. By lusting for the fruit of the tree of knowledge of good and evil, man was committing the sins of pride and greed by believing he could become equal to God and by seeking that which was beyond the provision of the creator. The temptation of Adam and Eve typifies temptation of the world.

In Jesus' forty days in the desert, we also see temptation of the flesh and temptation of evil spirits. In the flesh we have the basic instincts of man typified here by Jesus' need for bread or food. Actually, the temptation went beyond the need for food to the performing of an act of magic to satisfy his human need. Jesus here demonstrates that man can control his instincts through tapping into man's greater need of sustenance from God. "Man does not live by bread (food for the body) alone but by every word (food for the soul) that comes from the mouth of God."

In the second temptation, Jesus is being tempted by evil or untruth which originates from outside of man's self or the material world. Here his opponent is misapplying or wrongly interpreting the word of God. It's as if the enemy is using Jesus' source of strength, disclosed in the first temptation, against him. Very important here that Jesus does not correct his adversary. He does not resist evil. Instead he uses another weapon or scripture from his arsenal of truth. If Jesus threw himself down from a high place to demonstrate God's protection he would be misapplying a gift not intended to be applied in situations of self-glorification or self-abuse. In fact, if God did directly protect us against ourselves, He would be violating our free-will or going against His own immutable law. Instead, He gives us the tools we need to save ourselves from ourselves, the greatest of which is His Divine Love.

Here because Jesus is the living, human example of Divine Love, he easily sees the lie; and, rather than contradict it or argue or resist, he simply applies the truth, lives the truth, that we are not to tempt God. Thus he defeats this outside, cunning, deceitful evil not by focusing on evil but by focusing on his Father, the truth of his Father, and properly applying that truth; and we see that deceit cannot persevere when confronted with truth.

In the third temptation, the adversary is using the world again but differently than with Adam and Eve. Rather than trying to induce Jesus to seek equality with God, he attempts to flood his senses with desire for all the pleasures and riches of the world. He attempts to stimulate greed as with Adam but in a more tangible way. Jesus had already spurned material wealth, which, relatively speaking, was available to him if he had remained in his earthly father's trade, for the livelihood of an itinerant teacher. The enemy was probing what he perceived as a weakness. The lesson we take from this is we are more likely to be attacked in our areas of weakness. But through God we can turn our weakness into power.

Again, Jesus refused to focus on the pleasures available to him through a presented easier path. He refused to indulge in considering the temptation by focusing again on his Father, his real God, not the false gods offered by the world. These then are, as humans, our three sources of temptation working to pull us away from God: our flesh, the world, and evil spirits. When we yield to any of the three sources, we become out of harmony with God and his laws through which He orchestrates the universe. This is commonly called sin or separation from God.

The Greatest Power

In the late seventies, as I moved away from my involvement with the Cursillo movement and more toward focusing on the world, it's as if my spirit became dimmer and dimmer. By the late eighties, it seemed it had died which, of course, it can't; but it can become dormant. When this happens we ourselves are blocking our communication channels with God. But He never gives up on us and, like the father of the prodigal son, is always watching for our surrender, our turn back to Him and His forgiving heart.

Through our own strength or natural love we can determine that we will live in harmony with God's laws. Some are more successful than others in applying this; but, no matter how successful, with this method the struggle continues as long as we use our natural God-given strength, will-power, and love. Here the yoke is difficult and the burden heavy. This was my experience in my forty year struggle against my addiction. By changing to using God's strength instead of mine, I was able to defeat my enemy, that had been entrenched all those years, in less than forty days. My yoke became easy and my burden light by switching from my strength to God's strength, from my natural human love to God's all-powerful Divine Love.

This is what happens when our soul is reborn; and we receive the eyes of Jesus. We are transformed by God's Holy Spirit implanting the essence of God, the substance of God, His Divine Love in our souls. If man will but obey his Father, through the teaching of God's first divine son, he will be set free from all that can enslave him. We can see a strong parallel between Jesus and Moses who led the Israelites out of slavery in Egypt to the promised land of freedom. When Moses struck the sea with his staff, God parted the waters, their obstacle between slavery and freedom; and they passed through. Yet, they were not transformed for they were soon back to their old ways of worshipping idols.

Adam, or whom he represents, was created with the same capability to become divine as was Jesus; but Adam, through pride and greed, committed the first sin, the first severance of the umbilical cord between God and man, when he refused to obey and surrendered his freedom. Jesus, by his obedience and continuous focus on the Father, re-established this precious connection between mankind and God, gave us back our ability to accept God's offer of immortality; thus, as he claimed, he came to set the captives free, free from the bondage of habitual sin, free to choose the perfection of God living in and through us. Thus, according to Paul in the New Testament, we will be like Jesus, true sons and daughters of God, not in image only, but also in substance, in divinity.

The Second Coming

Today, many Christians are anticipating the impending second coming of Jesus in bodily form. They expect him to single-handedly eradicate sin from the face of the earth and establish his perfect rule. This cannot happen; for, here again, God would have to violate His immutable law which he will not do. God will not force man to stop sinning against his free-will. Man must choose to stop sinning and will eventually do so both on earth and in the spirit world. This will happen through the gentle persuasion of God and His angels and His human instruments on earth who are all helping us, working to influence us to the right path back to our Heavenly Father.

While Jesus' second coming in bodily form is not to happen, his second coming in spirit to the sphere of earth has already occurred; and its influence lingers with such as the writing of *40 Days to Freedom* and moreso this work. In fact, the primary purpose of this work is to integrate the teachings from his second coming with the previously known truth of God revealed through the *Bible* and other sacred scripture. To limit God's revelation of truth to the *Bible* alone is an injustice of man to both God and humankind and serves to limit man's progress toward the Father and knowledge of Him.

To know Him is to love Him. God's revelation to man is continuous. Man's ability to accept and absorb that revelation is limited by his own progress in that knowledge and his progress from imperfection toward the perfection desired for us by God and expressed by Jesus. God does not force perfection. He allows us to grow into it; and our growth is unlimited for all eternity; and, along with our perfection in the eyes of God, so too is our growth in our knowledge and understanding of Him; and, thus, also unlimited is the growth in the joy and peace which comes from this progress of humanity on its path to the All-Perfect Father of Creation.

So too is the progress of the one we call Jesus the Christ unlimited. According to the *Bible*, Jesus told us that the Father was greater than he and that the Father had not revealed everything to him. Jesus has again confirmed this revelation through his messages to mankind in his second coming. Why then do we insist on placing the impossible burden of being "God made man" on the shoulders of our savior after we crucified him? He, according to the *Bible*, never claimed such except through man's erroneous interpretation which is an injustice to God , to man, and to Jesus and tends to lessen the great sacrifice he made to give his message of freedom and the rebestowal of the gift of potential for intimacy and oneness with God.

Saying that Jesus' statement in response to the request from his apostle to show the Father was his declaration that he was God is wrong as he has declared in his second coming and in the *Bible*. It should be the statement of every child of God: "When you have seen me, you have seen the Father." Jesus reflected not only the image but the essence of God which is Divine Love. This is the perfection Jesus desires for all of us, a perfection seemingly impossible because of the erroneous teachings of the self-proclaimed representatives of God on earth. Their errors are understandable. Their manipulations of the truth for the sake of personal and institutional power were not of God. They have and will receive their just rewards, not imposed by an unforgiving god but imposed by the sins of their choosing and the law of retribution, we reap what we sow.

I, as a Catholic Christian, was not impressed with the suffering by crucifixion of the man I was taught was God through a doctrine developed by man which will remain for all time impossible for man to comprehend. After all, what would a few hours of physical pain mean to the God who knew everything?

When I was in the Air Force, I attended survival training in the Western US. I was placed in simulated life or death situations where I was expected to perform according to my training and survive which I did. But I had foreknowledge that I was not going to be allowed to die or abused in the tests. So it was easy. It wasn't real.

The impact of the glorious sacrifice made by Jesus to proclaim his truth, the truth about his Father, whom he defined as his God, never really touched me until I saw his humanity. For the first time, I saw it was a real man who suffered real pain and uncertainty as his humanity asked, according to the *Bible*, why his God had forsaken him. Jesus had suffered as I would suffer had I been in his place. He suffered for the truth and for the truth to set me free. Ironically, this teaching came from a bishop of the Catholic Church; for which I am grateful but also wish I had received in my youth instead of my thirties.

The Truth

What is the truth. The first definition in the dictionary is "a being true." As the Christ, the reflection of God, the expression of God through man, this definition is a perfect fit with the definition given by Jesus in the *Bible* when he said, "I am the way, the truth, and the life." This has become one of my favorite scriptures. But my very favorite is "God is love and he who lives in love lives in God and God in him." As the Christ, the soul of Jesus the man became the Divine Love, the Divine Essence, of God the Father. Adam had the same opportunity but, instead of reaching for oneness with the Father, instead of losing self in the Almighty, he sought self-glorification.

This then is the Christ Principle: to love God with all our heart and soul and mind and strength, with our entire being, to the extent we are seeking oneness with Him, to the extent we are seeking for His will to be our will, and to the extent, like Jesus, we are seeking to become love. Such desire and longing will never go unanswered by our Father.

If this is true, then Jesus is the very model of what we can become. If this is true, love is the way, love is the truth, love is the life. If this is true, we no longer have concern for our lives on this earth as our earthly circumstances are unable to dent our eternal well-being, our eternal peace, which, like Jesus and his apostles, we can even carry to the crosses we face in this life. The Apostles are the proof that this conversion was not reserved for Jesus alone as they were all converted, at least all but one, according to the *Bible*.

The Father's answer to our soul longing is always the same, to send His Holy Spirit, the carrier of His essence, His Divine Love, to us, to our souls, to imbue them with His Divine Presence for eternity. This then is the meaning of being "born again." This is the reason the soul of Jesus was incarnated and made man. This was the reason for his first coming two thousand years ago and for his second coming early in the twentieth century.

Let's stop for just a moment to consider this claim. Just what was different about Jesus two thousand years ago? Others had earlier come supposedly by virgin birth. Others were supposed to be man-gods. Others were great leaders and great teachers and displayed great wisdom. Blood sacrifice for sins was certainly not new. What was unique about Jesus?

No one else brought the message of spiritual rebirth to open the gates of heaven to humankind. Everything else he did, everything else he was, was secondary to this Divine Purpose. This also was the Great Commission he gave to his apostles, to spread his gospel, his message of the rebestowal of the offer of immortality from God to man. It was man who all but lost the primary message and taught more about Jesus' secondary message on moral living, do to others as we would have them do to us, love others as we love ourselves. The moral code he identified as the second greatest commandment and was tied to the natural love of man, the love that gives him the ability to survive on earth, a similar yet superior love to that of animals, but not divine.

Most of what Jesus taught about the rebirth was lost. It was too new, too radical. It was misinterpreted to show that faith in him as "the only begotten son of God" or leading a life of loving each other through good works or both was sufficient for the entry of a human soul to heaven. No amount of faith and no amount of good works can change mortal into immortal. Divinity is not given to man at his creation but is offered through his exercise of the unique and great gift of his free will. If he will seek, he will find.

This is why Jesus identified loving God as the first and greatest commandment and not with the same intensity that we love our neighbor but with all we have, all we can muster with our inferior love that at its best, as Paul defined, is slow to anger. Here again, we must pause to consider why we must love God with such intensity.

The answer goes back to the beginning, the beginning of humankind, the reason for the creation of man as described in the beginning of the *Bible*, the Book of Life, which tells us we were created to be the friends of God, which also points to the uniqueness of the creation of man separate from all else in creation. Man alone was given free will for the express purpose of choosing God as his friend. Think about this.

Evolution?

This is why the theory of man's evolution from lower animals can never be proved. The missing link will never be found because the physical realm cannot define man. The true man is not physical. The true man is soul in the image and likeness of God who is Soul. And God Soul made man soul to be his friend in love for eternity. This intended friendship is perhaps the greatest truth of the *Bible* because it is the core reason for everything else involving man. This highest creation of God, I believe, explains the very existence of all else in creation. And, if the true man, the real man, the man within the man, is soul, then what matter how God created the envelope of flesh which temporarily and very briefly encompasses the man within?

Reincarnation?

Now many believe that resurrection involves not only soul but also body. In a way this is true but incomplete. In his second coming early in the twentieth century, Jesus taught as you have here been reading. He further explained on this subject of creation that, when the soul of man is incarnated within the body of flesh, it also receives a spirit body, which it will occupy for the remainder of its existence. The body of flesh is the only part of man made to die and he occupies it only once. He has no further need for it or any body of flesh after his resurrection; and all men and women are resurrected, soul within spirit body after death on earth. The soul, through the spirit body, retains all the senses, memory, and intellect of the human. Each human being then consists of the three major parts: soul, spirit body, and physical body. That which is identified as spirit is the active energy of the soul and a part of the soul. The soul comes to earth to receive its individuality which it does no matter how short or how long the incarnation. There is no reincarnation as there is no purpose for it.

Some believe man progresses by living many lives in the flesh. Man progresses continuously throughout his one life in both the realm of earth and the realm of spirit. Probation and progression do not end with death of the flesh. There are many levels or spheres in the spirit world and the disincarnated soul within its spirit body enters the sphere of light or darkness for which it has been fitted by its life on earth. We will have more on this in the chapter on heaven and hell.

The Celestial Testament of Jesus
By now, the reader is perhaps asking, "What is the source of this new information I'm reading about Divine Love, rebirth, humanity versus deity of Jesus, evolution, reincarnation, etc.?" First, let me respond that I am simply sharing what I have learned over some sixty years of reaching for God. The reader realizes that my spiritual vision and learning capacity was impeded during the first fifty of those sixty years. This would be true not only of a moderate to orthodox lay Catholic Christian but also a priest educated in Rome or any *Bible* scholar or theologian living in the hell of habitual sin. What good if we are able to study all that has been written about God by man if we cannot connect with the *Internal Bible* given at our creation? If

our knowledge of God in our heads, our brains, never connects with or is challenged by our knowledge of God in our souls, then our study is for naught.

Perhaps, this would be the proper place to divulge my source of information about the second coming of Jesus. I have learned, especially since my rebirth in 1990, there are no coincidences; there is purpose in everything that happens. My youngest daughter was my full-time assistant since 1988. At that time, I was in the money business as a Certified Financial Planner. Peggy remained with me through the transition to Freedom Ministries, Inc. which started in late '94 and became our full-time endeavor in early '96. When she wasn't busy mailing books and newsletters, Peggy surfed the Internet to draw people to our web site. I had to let Peggy go in early '98 as I could no longer afford to pay her salary. More on how God purged me from financial self-reliance later.

One web site administrator responded to her inquiry after she left so, naturally, I received the message intended for her. He suggested a visit to his site as it had been recently improved. Had Peggy received this message, I probably would never have visited his site and would have missed the greatest boon to my spirituality since my rebirth. This is where I learned of Jesus' channeling messages through an attorney named James Padgett, who practiced law in Washington, DC, in the early nineteen hundreds. Mr. Padgett received some twenty five hundred messages from Jesus and other corroborating spirits from 1914 to 1923.

The method of transmission was referred to as automatic writing. Mr. Padgett testified in a letter to a friend that, as he wrote this information, he was only aware of the word being written. For sake of comparison, in my personal experience, I receive lines of thought that sometimes come so rapidly, it's difficult for me to type fast enough. I believe Mr. Padgett's experience to be a more pure form of communication, less subject to modification by the thoughts and beliefs of the medium. Of course, God and His angels are unlimited in their methods of communication with us. I suspect that Mr. Padgett's method requires a special gift, different from mine, which I fully appreciate without envy.

In fact, I am incredibly blessed by James' gift; and, through this work will share much of his revelation from Jesus in my own words and terminology, blended with the fruits of my gift, the eyes of Jesus, which, prior to discerning the Padgett Messages, had already contributed in the freeing and healing of countless souls through *40 Days to Freedom*.

The core of these blessed messages is a group of fifty-two referred to as *The Celestial Testament of Jesus*, or the New Gospel of Jesus. I encourage the reader to discern the information for himself at the same web site (www.divine.org) where I was led by, I believe, the orchestration of God. I confess I was greatly challenged in reading all fifty-two messages the first time as I found many corrections to what had been ingrained in me in my fifty years of Catholicism. Tradition and my intellect caused me to quit twice on my study before completion; but, each time, my *Internal Bible* brought me back.

I found answers to questions I had tried to subvert all my life because my religion told me that I didn't have to understand, just blindly accept, as if God was some magician closely guarding His secrets. I found just the opposite is true. He does want us to have faith; and, as Jesus reveals, even he is still growing and progressing in knowledge and oneness with the Father. The faith I now have is based on reason and understanding instead of unanswered questions of seeming contradictions.

In addition, I find all of the information to be confirmed by the *Bible*; and, yes, some of it could be disputed by other references to the *Bible*. Indeed, Jesus' stated reason for this transmission was to correct the modifications made to his message of two thousand years ago and not only his teachings but those of his apostles which were also changed. But, as he also revealed, the fundamentals of his message were preserved in the *Bible*. I personally find that the *Bible* makes a lot more sense after this enlightenment.

Revelation

By the way, the terminology *Internal Bible* I did not read

anywhere; nor have I ever heard it in any conversation or presentation. It was given by direct revelation where it first entered this writing. Some more versed in metaphysics may refer to it as direct or automatic writing, as with Mr. Padgett, where spiritual influence is so strong that, if the writer has the proper degree or attitude of surrender, it's as if the influence is using the brain of the writer to directly convey its message to the computer keyboard or the pen. I see it as divine revelation blended with everything of my sixty years experience in progressing to returning to my Father. This, I believe, is confirmed by my inspiration, "this is the reason," for my first book, *40 Days to Freedom*.

With this work as with my first, I claim my source of revelation to be the Spirit of the Living God. My basis for this claim is the presence which floods my senses during these early morning writings and when I daily study the Padgett Messages. It imparts a deep feeling of peace and love, being loved. In addition, the message, both in my writing and with Padgett, is always consistent with "God is love." This primary attribute of the Father Creator of all, I believe, is confirmed by the *Bible* and all my other sources of study He has directed me to over the past ten years since my spiritual rebirth.

In *40 Days to Freedom* I referred to the *Internal Bible* as the "basic operating system" given each of us at our creation and compared its value with the basic operating system of a computer. A computer without a basic operating system is useless, would just be a combination of plastic and glass and wire and electronics. It would be similar to a soul within the body of flesh and the body of spirit but with the spirit missing or dormant. This dormancy of spirit is experienced by too many in our world. It's as if most people are programmed to be educated in the way of the world, to become a materialist because "he who dies with the most wins." This quoted statement, which contradicts itself, I once saw as a bumper sticker. And, of course, this premise of materialism is an oversimplification; but we could substitute any of a myriad of modern, society-endorsed addictions.

Love

I don't believe, as we are taught, the love of money is the root of <u>all</u> evil; but it certainly accounts for a large share. I believe we need to go deeper to pride and greed and lust or combinations of the three; then, we can perhaps find the roots of all evil. Perhaps, if we look at their opposites of humility, selflessness, and control of our own mind we may find the roots of all good. Certainly they were all qualities of Jesus; and it would be difficult to imagine the practice of love without them.

Now here, considering the practice of love, we are tempted to think of doing good works which certainly is a manifestation of love but is not love itself. Good works can be done by man with his natural love, even with compassion; but these acts or manifestations of love for others will not create oneness with God, a dwelling in His abode, unless we become love; and, as Jesus told us the only way to that beginning is through spiritual rebirth or the imparting of the Divine Love of God into our souls by His Holy Spirit. This is what Jesus meant when he told us to be perfect as his our Heavenly Father is perfect. This is the Divine imbuing His highest creation with divinity in answer to sincere prayer and soul-longing.

When this really happens, whether you call it being born again, being saved, a spiritual awakening, being given the eyes of Jesus, whatever you call it, <u>you</u> <u>are</u> <u>transformed</u>. Paul in his writings referred to it as becoming a new creature and the scales dropping from his eyes. I think of the butterfly as a wonderful example God has given us in nature of what the potential is for each one of us. Am I talking here about anything so wonderful as becoming the President of the US, or a five-star general in the military, or a mega-billionaire in high-tech, or a top name in the arts? No, nothing so mundane as these!

I used to be envious of Jack Nicklaus, the professional golfer, who, at one time was the undisputed number one in his arena or profession. Jack and I are the same age; and, when he was at his career height, I too was hooked on golf but, at my best, about twenty strokes higher than him. I thought what he did was the epitome of a life of joy and fulfillment and freedom.

Now, don't get me wrong, one can be a born-again golfer or a born-again President, etc. The difference is the focus on what is really important, what really brings joy and peace and fulfillment and freedom. It has nothing to do with occupation. It has only to do with God living in and through us. Then, whatever the occupation, we'll do it better; not necessarily receiving more money, but always receiving more reward.

This is the only achievement worthy of the human being in the expression of our Creator. Then comes the goodness, the love, the service to mankind, not of ourselves but of God flowing through us, performing, if you will, His profession, His agenda, uniquely, according to His Divine Plan, through each one of us. This is the harmony for which He created man to live in a universe of harmony.

Freedom

Since my rebirth in 1990, I have learned much of and from the Father. My purpose in this work, through obedience, is to simply share that knowledge with the reader and, if it be God's will, in sharing to enlighten and make the reader's path to the Father and His Celestial Heaven a little easier. Also, God has revealed my purpose in all my writing in a single word is freedom. As I recently shared with a prison minister brother, I believe before my soul was incarnated, it was given the purpose of spreading freedom across the earth, of liberating souls from all that binds them to the confines of this solitary planet that they may soar free in God's Celestial Heavens.

It is not my expectation that every reader will agree with all he finds here; but, if each can remember something of what they read here as they pass from this world to the next, then the path will be made a little easier and the heart of my soul will be gladdened. My hope is that each reader will persist to the completion of reading this text for without such persistence, for which I claim no credit, I would not have been able to share this wonderful knowledge of the Father and His son and His spirit and His awesome Divine Love.

Boundaries of Discovery

From the standpoint of study material before my rebirth,

most of what nourished my soul could be considered traditional books including the *Bible*. Not that I hungered for knowledge of the Lord to the extent I now do; nor was my opportunity for study the same; though I could have made more time to learn of Him. In all those works I experienced the most enlightenment from those of Thomas Merton. A Catholic nun was the instrument through which I was introduced to Merton with my first exposure, The Seven Story Mountain, to which was added many of his blessed works. He was perhaps the first author to help me develop a conscious awareness of my *Internal Bible* when I recognized his writing of man's potential for oneness with God as if I had read it before. It was a connection I will never forget and for which I will be eternally grateful to Merton, for his surrender to become an instrument of God, allowing the Father to take him outside the boundaries of tradition.

If we are to grow in knowledge of God and closeness to Him, these boundaries must be broken. Religions and denominations tend to establish boundaries; but man's spirit was created free to remain free. So while religions can help us to connect, to communicate, and to worship, we should guard that they not become our gods as was the very situation disclosed by Jesus in his time on earth. Their boundaries tend to limit while God wants us unlimited in our oneness with and our enjoyment of Him.

So religion is useful when used to communicate with God especially when in unison with our brothers and sisters. Though, here again, when we break the boundaries of denomination, as I first experienced in prison ministry, the fellowship can soar to new heights. Indeed, the Kairos Prison Ministry teams that I have been privileged to work since 1992, have each allowed me to experience the bond of family where the uniting bloodline is an ecumenical love of God that allows us to set aside our doctrinal differences to serve his love-starved children in the prisons of the world.

This blessed interdenominational work has made, in its twenty-five year history, a substantial impact on the recidivism problem in America and is spreading its wonderful agape love to prisons throughout the world. I will forever be indebted to my Father for so obviously leading me to such a rich opportunity to experience the fulfillment of Jesus' mandate in Matthew 25 to love the unlovables of the world. He indeed expressed that these were the very people he came to set free.

Since my rebirth, God has provided me with study material both traditional and non-traditional. He has allowed me to see that, as with me, the work of most authors, imparting knowledge of Him to the world, including those of the *Bible*, is a mix of His inspiration with everything they have learned and experienced in their lifetimes so with each writer is a freshness of expression and a richness of experience to be shared with the reader. And, hopefully, with each work of the author is expressed a progression or growth in his own relationship with God which he shares with his audience in the hope that they too will grow in their individual relationships with their Creator. Thus man is enlightened and grows closer to God.

We see this in Christianity starting with the writers of the Old Testament and then with a progression of writers who dared to challenge the norms of their own Jewish Religion with writings inspired by a radical Jew, who had lived among them and taught them for a very short time; but who had a powerful impact on the world to the extent that the ripples of his message of the God of love are, two thousand years later, still inspiring writers and creating a tidal wave of information, in this age, that cannot be held back from reaching all peoples of the earth.

We see a progression in the authors, who have continued to write sacred scripture after the heroes of the *Bible*; for all writing, that adds to the freedom of humankind in progressing to oneness with the Creator of the universe, is indeed sacred scripture. To purport that God ceased to inspire the writings of man eighteen hundred years ago is not only absurd but an attempt to limit and control the God of no limitations and is itself blasphemy.

I have learned that God wants each of us to constantly grow in both our relationship with Him and our knowledge of Him. It seems to me each feeds the other; and our growth in relationship is fed not only by study but also by prayer and experience. Certainly all three led to my growth and to my rebirthing experience. Through these three, we realize the truth in the statement, "to know Him is to love Him."

Once Saved Always Saved?

This growth doesn't mean we always become more liberal in our view of the characteristics of the Almighty. For example, the Catholic perspective, ingrained in me from birth, is contrary to the concept of "once saved always saved." I used to argue enthusiastically with my Protestant brothers and sisters against this concept and considered my most powerful argument was Jesus' teaching in the *Bible* that those who remain strong in faith and love to the end will be saved.

Through the Padgett Messages, I learned that, once we receive the Divine Love of God in our souls, it can never be replaced by that which is not divine. In other words, once divine always divine and with divinity comes immortality. Therefore, from the moment of that implanting by the Holy Spirit of the substance of God in our souls, we are irrevocably marked for heaven, the domain of the Most High. The logic, reason, and, most of all, confirmation by my *Internal Bible* of this concept, given by Jesus to Mr. Padgett, was so powerfully received by my soul that I had to accept it both as the truth and as wonderful news.

Jesus also related, however, that if the reborn soul subsequently strayed from the light back into darkness, even though the Divine Essence remains, it will not displace the free will of man. This law of non-manipulation God will not violate while man is man; therefore, it is possible for the saved soul, after passing from the physical world to the spiritual, to experience darkness before entry to the Celestial Heavens of God. Before entry into the domain of the divine, probation is continuous both in the physical and spiritual realms. The soul does not enter the Celestial Heavens before reaching the degree of perfection in the Divine Love as determined only by God; then the final transformation from human to Divine Angel. Again, once born again, man's destiny is heaven as the Divine

Angel.

This final transformation is the most glorious of all; for, then, the soul, the person, has full knowledge, beyond faith, of his divinity and immortality. Also, here is the transformation of the human free will into the will of God. This, then, is what every Christian is aiming for and, not only every Christian, but every person on earth who is seeking oneness with God. Perhaps, Jesus did say, "The only way to the Father is through me." But he certainly did not say, "The only way to the Father is by proclaiming yourself a Christian." Jesus was love incarnate. The "way" he referred to is the way of love.

I have also learned, through the study of the Padgett Messages, that God is a benevolent God; for, without having this precise knowledge, many souls have reached the Celestial Heavens. So with our Father, we don't have to be one hundred percent correct, just one hundred percent sincere. In other words, we can't con our way into heaven; nor will intellectual knowledge alone provide entrance. Also, by this, we can see we can't make a death-bed conversion after a life of sin and then, after body death, expect to awake in heaven. Those who teach such a false concept will experience the same rude awakening as their students or perhaps worse. Only divinity can become one with Divinity; and God alone decides when the imperfect becomes the perfection of the Divine Angel.

Sacred Life

The last thing I would like to say in this chapter on being born again deals with life itself and the human perspective of life. While working on this chapter, I attended a conference in Arizona on Christian Meditation and was privy to some of the philosophy of Houston Smith, the guest speaker of three days. He proposed that the ruling authority of this day is "scientism" which ignores that which is spiritual. I believe this to be true and, indeed, indicative of the ignoring of the spiritual life which precedes, includes, and follows this physical life on earth.

Recently, I was shocked when the moderator and founder of a prominent news and talk show on Christian TV put forth his opinion that the USA should assassinate the man believed to be the preeminent funder of world terrorism, especially against the United States; and, in the next breath, stated we should also conduct a preemptive strike against North Korea because of their developing potential to conduct a nuclear or chemical warfare strike against us. Though I had disagreed with this man before on the death penalty issue and had written without response, I could hardly believe my ears. In fact, his co-host seemed shocked at his animate assertion which he quickly defended, as legalized killing, not in conflict with the *Bible*. It appears to me such a premise has been used to justify many wars including some of Hitler's preemptive strikes against its neighbors in World War II.

But more than this, what occurred to me was Jesus' teaching that, if we endeavor to save our lives, we will lose them which, I believe, pertains here with our focus on this physical life as most important. Even if we profess to believe in life after death, our confusion, contributed to by the disparity between religions and denominations, about what to expect erodes our confidence. Our society is not only focused on preserving and extending physical life but, perhaps, equally focused on preserving our way of life including that which is perceived as freedom and affluence. God doesn't object to our enjoying His many gifts as long as we share them with others which is what love is all about. He does object to our making His gifts to us our gods. This worship of materialistic idols in America today is rampant. In addition, we seem unwilling to trust God's protection in national issues. Our faith in our Father's love is greatly lacking.

We also see this in the raising and educating of our young with the proportion of time spent on preparing them to live the physical life and little or no time preparing for the spiritual, which lasts forever, including the time on this earth. Thus we see not only those who are identified as Christian news and talk show hosts justifying murder, but also our youth, usually without moral or spiritual values through no fault of their own, actually murdering their peers and teachers.

The teaching of Jesus was just the opposite of the hawkish approach of some Christian leaders of today. He taught the resolution of these and all problems through love, even loving our enemy. But he didn't teach during an age of atomic bombs and chemical warfare. So here again, we become fixed on preservation of our own lives as the justification to murder others which is flawed in any age. I wonder what would happen if we provided love in the form of food in abundance to starving North Korea without any strings attached. More important than the lessening of physical threat, how would God see this; and how might He respond?

When truly born again, there is no longer any stomach for violence against any of God's creation; and, with the eyes of Jesus, we gain insight into his statements, that previously seemed so difficult to understand and live, such as love of enemy and light burden and being perfect in and giving rather than saving one's own life. God is so awesome. The greatest gift He gives us next to life itself is freedom, a gift that was thrown away by Adam and Eve, or who they signify, and was rebestowed through Jesus of Nazareth. And to me, God is most awesome in His simplicity; for, as Jesus taught, all we have to do to receive the greatest freedom of new life in oneness with God is ask; and Jesus promises we shall receive.

This new life, which I experience as heaven on earth, was undoubtedly the greatest gift I have received in my lifetime. I now understand the zeal of the Apostles, after their rebirth, after Pentecost, that even body death was no obstacle to performing their great commission. The continuing of Jesus' work, especially since it was so misunderstood, is not without great risk. The risk to me may not be literal crucifixion but rather crucifixion in the minds of many dear to me. Yet the reward, not for me, for I already have it, but for those I love, is potentially so great to be worth the risk of alienation.

If the reader will simply dare to complete the reading of this work, my purpose is then fulfilled. If he leaves this work, I pray his *Internal Bible* will cause him to return to its completion. God has given me an awareness that, if only this is accomplished, the path to the Celestial Heavens of the Father, for those who persist, will be made more visible and easier.

Thank you, Father, for giving me heaven on earth and the privilege of serving You.

IV. PASSION

The Second Man

Passion is defined as "the suffering of Jesus during the crucifixion or after the Last Supper." I must admit to being very surprised to find this as the first definition given. These definitions followed: "2. any emotion ....., 3. extreme emotion ....., 4. the object of strong desire or fondness." Entering my Webster's New World Dictionary, I expected the last of these to be first. Certainly, we can see that the last definition is very contrary to the first in that Jesus demonstrated the opposite of desire to be crucified. The Gospel is clear that, as the hour of his arrest drew near, his fear of impending crucifixion was so great that he sweat blood.

Now some might believe that such a bizarre claim of the Gospel, as sweating blood, to be made up for effect. I believe just the opposite is true. Though I have never known of any such occurrence, I have learned that it is real enough to have been given the medical name hematidrosis. The fear or trauma, experienced by Jesus in the garden before his arrest, was so severe that the capillaries in his sweat glands burst causing him to literally sweat blood. I cannot fathom that this would be made up by anyone especially in reference to the son of God who was otherwise portrayed as fearless. No, I believe it happened and was probably witnessed. This, by the way, also fits the third definition of the word passion so this is where we will begin our look at the suffering part of Jesus' passion.

Jesus the Man

But, even before this, we must first look at exactly who this Jesus of Nazareth was. As earlier shared, until my Cursillo experience, I regarded Jesus as simply the son of God and, therefore, God, as one of the three persons in the trinity of the one God, as I had been taught by my church. Though aware, I didn't give a lot of thought or attention to the passion of Jesus probably because subconsciously I didn't relate to the Almighty God experiencing physical pain from torture.

But this attitude changed when I accepted that Jesus experienced what any man would experience in his place. I accepted that somehow his powers as God were blocked so this could be. This certainly appeased my puzzlement at his weakness in the garden and on the cross when he asked why God had forsaken him. And, no, I have never accepted that he said that just to fulfill Old Testament Scripture. I don't believe Jesus ever said anything he didn't mean. Further, I believe, now more than ever, he is the truth in God's human expression.

Now let's get back to the blocking of his powers as God. Certainly, for God all things are possible; but that doesn't mean he characteristically does the impossible or performs magic. And, even if Jesus could block these God powers, are we to assume that he did so he could suffer as a human and for what purpose? That's right! Christianity tells us it was for the purpose of paying for our sins, past, present, and future; but only for Christians because the rest of the world is going to hell.

Anger and Wrath of God?

And to whom was this ransom paid and why? Right again! Paid to an angry god whose anger could only be appeased by his son's torture and murder, his blood sacrifice. In fact, we are asked to accept that God the Father perpetrated this whole passion situation because He loves us so much except, of course, for those who refuse to accept this ridiculous scenario as their only path to salvation, which still translates to most of those in the world going to hell, no matter how good, how loving, how selfless they are. And, of course, we must consign, by God's own design, Judas and the religious leaders, whom He predestined to act out their nefarious roles, to the same fiery consequence. And what about Pilate and the soldiers and the members of the angry crowd? Well I guess we'll have to ask our religious leaders of today to determine God's judgment for them. Please, folks, don't lay this on the One, that in our next breath, we call Love.

Yes, a ransom was paid but not to an angry, unforgiving god. The ransom price, the suffering of Jesus the Christ, was paid to those who were threatened by his continuing life on earth. How could their silly rituals and impossible rules be justified if the doctrine of this radical Jew was believed by the masses? Their jobs and cushy lifestyles would certainly be affected; but, worst of all, they would lose their power over the people. There is a saying about power corrupting "absolutely." Jesus taught one rule, one law, love. God simplifies and man complicates; and so it has always been. This could not be tolerated by the Pharisees and Sadducees so Jesus had to pay the price for them to stay in power.

Yet, the church he founded survived. Initially, it was a simple society of love for God and one another. But, here again, man had to complicate for whatever reason. Perhaps the young church wasn't growing fast enough or perhaps it was threatened. Certainly in those very early years, many people saw the light of Jesus' teaching of non-violence and self-sacrifice with knowledge of a better life in the next world as so many gave their lives rather than deny their faith in the God of love and the messiah He sent. Certainly this can only be explained if these selfless people, like the Apostles, had truly been reborn into new creatures. This power of love taught by Jesus as the way the truth and the life soon even conquered Rome as it claimed Christianity as the official religion.

Is Jesus God?

But, as the decades and early centuries went by and word of mouth was written, then copied, then translated, then copied, with each transcriber destroying the material he copied, error and change were incorporated into the sacred texts. Now, some would say this cannot be so; there can be no error in the inspired word of God in the *Bible*. I must disagree that error and change must be so, as it is human nature; and God will not manipulate man. There is not one instance reported in the *Bible* of God forcing man to do anything. As soon as He violates man's free will, whether man's will results in unintentional error or intentional manipulation for purpose, then there is no human free will; and there is no possible friendship with God chosen by man; there is only slavery.

In those early centuries, a decision was made by man, not

God, that Jesus was to be God and the Trinity was invented, or I should say copied, by the Christian Church as this doctrine had its roots in early East Indian religions as did the concept of virgin birth. Perhaps it was feared if Jesus was seen as a mere man, though a very special man, the church's survival would be threatened.

Jesus never claimed to be God. Over and over, according to the *Bible*, he referred to himself as the "son of man." Over and over, he identified God as "the Father." The *Bible* quotes him saying, "the Father is greater than I." A "veil" it was explained separated the son from the Father so he could not see his equality which thus motivated this false statement from the one identified as "the truth." This "veil" then could also explain Jesus' true suffering not as God but as "fully" man. There is just one flaw in this reasoning created by men who tell us we should not reason but just blindly believe. They would have us believe that Almighty God would appease man's centuries earlier created myth of lifting of sin through burnt offerings or scapegoats or blood sacrifices by taking revenge on His one and only "begotten" son and that this was the primary purpose for sending him into the world. Jesus himself refuted this ridiculous fabrication with the parable about the wicked tenants who abused or killed first the servants, signifying the Old Testament prophets, and then the son, signifying Jesus, of the landlord, signifying God. The landlord father obviously did not send the son for the purpose of being killed; nor would any father.

Make no mistake, Jesus is the son of God; but that doesn't make him God. He is the son in two ways: first, he is a human soul created by the Father, as you and I; and, second, he was the first son to be born again by receiving the Divine Love Essence of the Father which transformed his soul from mortal to divine. In this latter sense, when he walked this earth, he was truly the "one and only" son of God; but also truly, as Paul later wrote, he was the first of many sons; and, when the Christ Essence, which is the Divine Love of the Father, takes residence in our souls, as it did with Jesus, through God's Holy Spirit, we become like Jesus, divine sons and daughters of God, though not equal to him as he is not equal to the Father. Neither is the Holy Spirit of God an equal part of the trinity, but an expression or emissary of the Father whose purpose is the imbuing of the Divine Love into the souls of humans.

Faith and Reason

Much of this clarification of Scripture came to me as a result of studying the Padgett Messages for well over a year, at this writing, on an almost daily basis. I have found faith based on reason to be much stronger than blind faith, and indeed a faith that one would be willing to die for. I, as I would imagine would be the case with many Christians, would not cherish the thought of facing an angry, vengeful, unforgiving god who orchestrated the brutal death of his only son. God has not allowed the progress in the development of human spirit and intellect for us to remain lodged in the creations of myth of ancient, fearful man predating Christianity and even Judaism. Man's progression toward oneness with the God of Love is stymied by such foolishness. It is, at last, time that we stop trying to remake God in our image; and that we allow Him to remake us in His image. This surrender, to the only true freedom that exists for humanity, man has stubbornly fought almost since his creation.

Here, I would be surprised if at least some readers were not only shocked at these proclamations but were feeling empathy for the soul of this writer committing seeming blasphemy against religious tradition and thus consigning himself to eternal damnation. I could only respond, if at this point any reader still feels it possible for any human to be allowed to experience that judgment by violating any law created by the God of Love, in prayer that this reader will be given the eyes of Jesus, the eyes of truth, the eyes of love.

This issue will be covered in greater detail in the chapter on heaven and hell; but I might offer this comparison as an inducement for the reader to continue his study here. I have a daughter who has denied my existence for about eight years. I am blessed that my ex-wife of twenty-three years, our four grown children, and their children all live in my local area so we have family gatherings with all in attendance more frequently than the average dispersed family. For eight years this daughter has refused to talk with me, look at me, or otherwise acknowledge that I exist when we attend these gatherings or elsewise.

There is nothing that this beloved daughter can do to make me love her any more or any less. She is my child; this is irrevocable fact; and I love her equally as I do her sisters and brother. I do pity her, as I know she is suffering greatly from her behavior, in the same way I believe God pities any of His children who stray from the way of love. I would not consign her to eternal damnation for any reason; and my love is as a thimble-full in comparison to God's love as an ocean. She does have the potential to give me more joy than my other children, through reconciliation, as the prodigal son and as the one lost sheep of the hundred.

The *Bible* tells us that God's will is that none be lost; yet Christianity presents the sacrifice of the many for the few. No, I'm wrong because all are permitted to join this exclusive club by proclaiming Jesus as their savior if they will just accept these contradictory doctrines which make no sense; but that's okay because we're not supposed to understand God. Is it any wonder that Christianity is the most splintered of all religions? Is it any wonder that of the estimated 1.6 billion people, who identify themselves as Christians, an estimated one seventh attend church regularly; and, among those, how many are attending because they really want to express love for the Father, and how many for other selfish purpose or threat of sin judgment if missed? Is it any wonder, as reported on the 700 Club during this writing, that every month fifteen hundred ministers are leaving ministry?

In this work, not the work of a *Bible* scholar or theologian but a freed addict, I can only tell you what I have come to believe and identify my sources of study, which I believe to be reasonable, though fundamental or orthodox Christians might claim them otherwise or even disagree that reason should be blended with faith. I believe God gave humans the gift of reason

82

for a purpose; and I believe our reasoning power is tied to our *Internal Bible*, our built in knowledge of God, as is our conscience. I'm not saying the *Internal Bible* is a direct source of knowledge to our conscious minds but more of a confirming source when we are exposed to the truth through seeing or hearing or other spiritual methods of revelation.

Who is Jesus?

I can tell you who I believe Jesus to be based on my eyes of Jesus (rebirth), my study, my *Internal Bible*, revelation from God and His angels, and my reasoning powers. I believe Jesus is a soul, created in heaven by the One he identified as his Father and our Father, his God and our God. To that we could reasonably add his Creator and our Creator. Therefore, since I believe the soul to be the real person, as taught by Jesus in the Padgett Messages, I believe Jesus, in the spiritual sense, which is more real than the physical, to be my brother. As with you and me, he was created to serve God and man in a special, unique way, yet with a free will that would not be violated by his Father.

One of my favorite passages in the *Bible* is at the beginning of the Gospel of John where he refers to "the Word became flesh." I believe "the Word" to be love. As His primary attribute and, as best we can understand, even the substance of God, love has always been. It is this Divine Love then that became flesh but not at Jesus' birth as many misinterpret but at his rebirth when he was baptized by his cousin John and the Holy Spirit of the Father.

I believe his earthly parents were Joseph and Mary. This is confirmed by Old Testament prophesy about the Messiah being in the line of King David, which Joseph was, not Mary. I believe he was taught and ministered to by Hebrew teachers and angels and God. I believe he grew to manhood without sin.

I believe Jesus frequently, if not constantly, sought oneness with God and was the first human being to receive the Divine Essence of God in his soul thereby becoming the Christ, the Messiah, the human expression of God on earth, and love incarnate. I believe him to be the epitome of the way, the truth, and the life. I believe he was the first inhabitant of the Father's Celestial Heavens, and, though rare, as he teaches through Padgett, was so filled with the Love of the Father that he became divine while on earth.

I believe, as the *Bible* relates, that, after his death, Jesus visited all the spirit world and announced the good news of the rebestowal of the gift of potential for immortality for all humans living on earth or who had ever lived on earth from the highest heavens (not the Celestial Heavens) to the lowest hells of the spirit world. Yes, potential, because immortality, oneness with God, friendship with God, as taught and modeled by Jesus, must be sought and will not be forced by the Father. Jesus sought his baptism by John and the Father; and, since this all-important event in the history of humanity and Jesus' subsequent announcement to Nicodemus and the spirit world, to every person who has sincerely sought, with deepest, heart-felt desire, this same oneness with the Father, it has been granted; and this is how they have found "the way" to "the life" in "the truth" proclaimed by Jesus as in the *Bible* and Chapter Three of this work.

I believe Jesus has come to earth again, not in physical body form, but in spirit form; and my *Internal Bible* confirmed the truth of the messages he gave to James Padgett early in this century. I believe, through this present work, ordained by the Father, Jesus' second coming continues in the transmission of those messages in the language of the land that will again be "of the free and home of the brave" entering the Third Millennium.

We speak here not of physical freedom, which is inconsequential in comparison to the spiritual freedom I am blessed to experience and as I have seen modeled by joy-filled prisoners, who will never again know the physical freedom taken for granted by most Americans; yet, unlike most, they are truly free and give thanks to God for the imprisonment which led to their freedom.

This is the man I know as Jesus the Christ, the first divine son of God, lord of the living and the dead as proclaimed by Paul in the *Bible*, savior, master, the true harbinger of freedom to the world.

The Ultimate Pacifist

After his sweating of blood during prayer in the garden, we know Jesus was arrested. According to the *Bible*, Peter came to his defense and was rapidly admonished by Jesus referring to "the cup" he was given by his Father. We are to believe by "the cup" he was referring to the cross; but this is not so as we have presented. Instead "the cup" referred to the way of non-violence and non-resistance to evil. Through all his passion of suffering, we see Jesus, though physically weakened starting with the hematidrosis and progressing with each abuse after his arrest, remaining focused on his Father and the way of love.

There is a much abused passage in the *Bible* about Jesus, upon entering the temple in Jerusalem, fashioning a whip, driving animals from his Father's house, and overturning tables. The abuse is using this single incident to try to portray a violent Jesus which is totally inconsistent with everything else we see demonstrated by this man of love. I believe Jesus demonstrated anger, which is not of the Divine Love of God but rather of the natural love of man, which he also possessed, being "fully man." But there is no evidence that he used the whip for other than the animals and then only to drive them from the temple.

Jesus was the ultimate pacifist. The Jews expected a warrior messiah; but they got the opposite, the man of love from the God of Love who taught us to love our enemies and do good to those who persecute us. We, even as professed Christians, after two thousand years, still haven't learned his lesson and try to twist it to suit our own selfish desires. We persist in trying to portray a god of violence and vengeance, who sent His only son to a horrible physical death, thereby violating His own commandment given to Moses. Well, He didn't! Instead, Jesus chose to fight violence with non-violence, with non-resistance, with love, love of his Father and love of his brother, no matter how gross the acts of the brother, forgiving his very executioners, again, focusing on the Father, portraying the Father, in whom is no unforgiveness.

The Body and Blood of Jesus

Love is the food of life. It is through love that God provides our physical food, real food for our physical bodies. It is through love that He provides our spiritual food, Jesus the Christ, real food for our souls. This is what Jesus meant when he said, "My body is real food and my blood is real drink." I drew this conclusion after meditating on what a friend recently related he had learned about cannibalism, which professes the mythic belief that the one eating was receiving the desirable attributes, such as the ability to run fast, of the one being eaten. Jesus' body and blood, in sacrifice that we might know the truth, became real food and real drink not for our physical bodies but for our souls. They are the nourishment we commemorate with Eucharist or communion of bread and wine. As love incarnate, his food for us was indeed his love. The belief that his sacrifice somehow magically removes our sins is totally myth and totally the invention of man stemming from a much earlier time.

Without Jesus' surrender to the cross, he would have denied the truth he taught about the greatest gift God can give to man, immortality through the New Birth through the Holy Spirit in the Divine Love of God, and the greatest gift man can give to man, love unto death. His sacrifice didn't take our sins away; we can't pass that obligation to another, to a "scapegoat." We can only use the means God provides to come back into harmony with His laws. When we are out of sync with His laws, we are in hell where we will remain until, through the ministrations of God and Jesus and the angels, we leave our baggage of sin behind in the darkness of hell and come into the glorious light of God. This will be presented in greater detail in a later chapter.

We must return to this man-god or god-man issue. The Apostles did not see Jesus as God but they did see God in Jesus. Is this an important distinction? If we worship Jesus the man as God, we are committing idolatry. If we worship Christ which is the Divine Love of God, God's very essence in Jesus, then we are closer to the truth. But, if we worship the Father as Jesus instructed "in spirit and in truth," then we are right on target. Jesus does not want our worship and never asked for it. When

Jesus sought our belief not that he is God but that he is truth. How do we know he is truth? He taught love; he defined love; he lived love; he was love incarnate. He was the demonstration of what John later wrote, "God is love and he who lives in love lives in God and God in Him." And Paul expressed the same when he wrote, "It is no longer I who lives but Christ who lives in me."

The Physical Proof

We now invite you to examine and contemplate the face and body of the crucified Jesus, the man, who gave himself in a most terrible death, that the truth might live in and through man. Christ, the Divine Love of God, did not die on the cross; but Jesus the man, the carpenter turned teacher and healer, did. This was not his desire as his agony is a matter of record. Certainly, no one could have concocted the trauma that caused his sweating blood which would weaken his strong body, intensify his suffering from the torture to follow, and hasten his expiration on the cross. We submit, for the discernment of your *Internal Bible*, the flawless pictorial Gospel of Jesus, created by the One identified in the *Bible*, Who raised him, with the only assistance from man being unaltered photography.

I will not here present scientific evidence of the authenticity of the Shroud of Turin. There are many authors and scientists who have gone far beyond my capabilities in that regard. In addition, this work is a sharing of my life and what I have learned, as a born-again Catholic Christian, and not a scientific presentation. Science is both baffled and challenged by this perfect, faint image of a crucified man on burial linen. Though it admits inability to recreate the process, it speculates the cause of the scorched image on only the very top filaments of the cloth fibers to be heat or light or radiation or a combination.

Because, perhaps, of my military background, one comparison has stuck in my mind. It likened the process to an atomic explosion, from within the body within the cloth, for one millionth of a second which, to me, clarifies its supernatural origin as being the only possibility. I offer no proof other than the sources already discusssed. At the end of one of many television presentations on the Shroud, the statement was made, "For some, there will never be enough proof. For others, no proof is necessary."

I have been a student of the Shroud since the late 1980's. When I first saw the image of the face on a book cover, I knew I was looking at the face of Jesus; and I knew it was authentic before reading the first word of evidence. Of the hundreds of tests done on the cloth and the image, only one pointed to inauthenticity; and that one did not affect my belief. It did however affect my including Shroud information in my first book. After completing and reviewing the manuscript, I was concerned that it might detract so I prayed for guidance. The answer came rapidly in what I believe was the first published scientific report repudiating the use of the carbon test with this linen material.

Indeed new evidence has come to light even since the latest published book on the subject. I would caution the reader, who studies the scientific data, that it is the imperfect work of man as we have previously discussssed and, therefore, cannot be without error. If you approach the wealth of data written on the Shroud, as we have suggested you approach the *Bible*, looking at the whole, at the pattern, at the progression of truth, rather than insisting that every test be perfect, then, we believe, you will be both fascinated and blessed as has this writer. We caution, though science seems to rule with much authority in this age, that it too is subject to the imperfection of man. God alone is perfect; and, if you, as I, accept the Shroud of Turin as the production of the hand of God without the assistance of man, then we are both blessed by this gift from a loving Father to the doubting Thomases of the world, a perfect Gospel of the Truth, written by God alone, which has survived wars, fires, and other threats from both man and nature to be read by you this day. This is why the Shroud is important, not that it can be ogled or venerated as some other simple icon or relic, as a left-over from a gone era, but for the story it tells with the accuracy of any modern-day photograph.

The image itself has been compared to a photographic

negative which seemed to come to life when, in 1898, Secondo Pia viewed the glass plates from his first session with the Shroud. It was as if he was looking at a negative of a negative which created the positive image of the face of Jesus (Page101) his eyes were the first to see. For the first time, the tortured body of Jesus (Pages102 and 103) could be seen with every wound and every blood flow clearly depicted. If indeed a fake, why would the creator make such a faint image so difficult to view without photography which was still centuries away from invention?

Prayer and Meditation

We will now ask the reader to study and meditate on the wounds shown on the images as we correlate them to the written Gospels. Here, as elsewhere in this work, we are primarily quoting scripture from memory and are therefore paraphrasing without reference to chapter and verse. The reader is free to validate our assertions with the use of a concordance and *Bible*. We do not intend to use the *Bible* to validate the Shroud but the opposite. We will present only photographic negative images as this is where we experience the greatest pictorial definition of information. And we will begin with the top of the image, front and back of the head of Jesus.

With each description, I will ask you to turn to the appropriate photograph and meditate on what you see. After the presented meditation and prayer with each wound comment, I ask that you close your eyes and listen to your inner voice, to what God has to say to you. If a message or prayer comes into your mind, don't resist it; let it flow. Take your time. When you are finished with your meditation and prayer, return to this text for the next comment about the image. If you find you must let some time pass before returning to the text, that's all right. Allow the Father to be in control of your time, your meditation, and your prayer. You will be richly blessed. And now, we begin.

Thorn Wounds:

You see above the left eyebrow (Pages 101 and 102) what appears to be a number three. This is blood flow from a crown of thorns that was more like a helmet than the ringlet often depicted in art. You will note several other light marks of similar intensity over the top and down the back of the head (Page 103) to about ear level showing multiple blood rivulets caused by the thorns. You will recall that, according to the Gospels, Jesus received this crown after his scourging and they ridiculed him saying, "Hail, king of the Jews;" and they hit him on the head. The image gives evidence that he was, indeed, hit on top of his crown of thorns for the obvious purpose of driving them deeper and causing more pain.

Meditation:

Brother Jesus, this crown of thorns, mocking your kingship, was placed on your precious head early in your passion and remained until after you had breathed your last. As if your torment would not be enough to satisfy your accusers, they clubbed your helmet of thorns to drive them deeper through the hair and flesh of your precious head. This price you paid for teaching love while your adversaries taught ceremonies and rules. This price you paid that all might see the truth about your Father, the God of Love; yet, now as then, we have eyes that do not see and ears that do not hear. Perhaps now, that I may see the results of the thorns piercing your head and spilling your blood, perhaps now, my eyes and ears will be opened to your truth for the first time. You taught a message of loving one's neighbor as oneself, of being meek, of accepting persecution for righteousness, and of focusing on oneness with the Father, instead of focusing on our problems in this world. Here, Jesus, you live what you taught. Thank you, Brother Jesus, for teaching and living the truth.

Prayer:

Our Father, thank You for sending Jesus with Your message of love. Thank You for the courage and strength You gave him to endure the trials and punishment from his adversaries for Your cause. Remove, we beg You, all the thorns of rebellion and greed and lust and selfishness from our hearts and minds. Father, give us his courage, his strength, his love that we might endure all life's challenges with our focus firmly fixed on You; for You are our refuge, You are our Source of strength, You are our Source of provision, and, above all, You are Love. Amen.

Facial Wounds:

A large swelling bellow the right eye (Page 101), a swollen nose, possibly broken, a triangular shaped abrasion on the right cheek, and swelling of both eyebrows probably resulted from multiple causes sited in the Gospels, starting with being hit in the face during his trials, continuing as he walked through the angry mob as they spit on him as well as hit him, and also resulting from falling on his face while carrying the instrument of his death.

Meditation:

Jesus said that every teacher, who had been instructed about the Kingdom of God, brought forth from his storeroom new treasures as well as old. He was that teacher. His storeroom was his *Internal Bible* stimulated and nourished by the Father and His angels who taught Jesus the truth which he in turn taught us. But the religious leaders, then as now, said there could be no new truth; and, to stay mired in their old ways of myth and tradition and protect their power over the people, they manipulated the government to kill you. Yet, you had found the priceless treasure, the knowledge of God, that is buried in every man and the pearl of wisdom, which says that God is our source of all that is good and right and true, so you gave the greatest gift man can give to man, to show man the way, the truth, and the life which is not in the flesh but in the spirit.

Prayer:

Father, we praise you and we thank you for sending Your son of Your loving heart to save us from our sin and error. We thank you for Your loving heart that sent Jesus with the message that you had reestablished the way to you refused by Adam and his descendants, the way of obedience and surrender and love. Help us, Father, to stop spitting in Your son's face. Help us to see, with the eyes of Jesus, Your great love for each and every one of us in spite of our abuse of your gifts and our stubborn refusal to listen to and live by Your son's message. Amen.

Scourge Wounds:

The Roman flagrum was much more than a simple whip. Extending from the handle were two or more leather thongs with lead miniature dumbbells affixed to the ends for the purpose of gouging flesh and producing profuse bleeding. Dumbbell shaped wounds cover both the front and back images (Pages 102 and 103) on the Shroud and depict that Jesus was naked when scourged, was probably tied to a post with his hands above his head, and two soldiers, one on either side, conducted the beating. The *Bible* gives reference to the flogging or scourging of Jesus and also to his "stripes" which, indeed, seems applicable to the crossing patterns of these horrible wounds.

Meditation:

Jesus, it is as if you are making a statement here, that the truth is worth any cost, any penalty is preferable to a lie; but, then, you told us you are "the truth." I believe you Jesus; and my *Internal Bible* believes that you taught the truth when you walked this earth and, again, early in this century, through James Padgett. I believe you are the first divine son of God, soul in the image of Soul, made Divine Love in the essence of the Father through His Holy Spirit. Yes, I believe that in you a part of God Himself, the Creator, the Father, walked this earth in your flesh because, as you taught, it is His desire that none will be lost. And, you taught us this is possible, through the free will of man, if man will seek oneness with the Father with all his heart, with all his soul, with all his mind, and with all his strength. Only this way, the way of Jesus, the way of sincere seeking, can we draw the response of the Holy Spirit and, as the *Bible* tells us, become like him, true sons and daughters of the Father in image and in substance.

Prayer:

Heavenly Father, would that I could open the eyes of all your people that they may see the truth You have revealed to me, the same truth Jesus died for, rather than deny, the truth that says You love each of us as if we were Your only child, no matter what we look like, no matter what we've done, no matter what we believe. But they turn away, Father. They believe in the lies of the world that tell them it's too hard, too much to sacrifice; and they turn away. Their eyes are on the world with all its problems and its false gods. I pray, Holy Father, that each will be given the eyes of Jesus, that they may see that You are the only freedom for humankind and that the ultimate freedom You offer every one is oneness with You. Amen.

Shoulder and Back Abrasions:

On the right shoulder (Page 103, back image) and left shoulder blade patches of abrasions can be identified. According to John's Gospel, Jesus carried the cross (patibulum) to Golgotha where he was executed. From these abrasions and the damage to his face from falls, scientists have estimated the weight of the beam tied to his arms across his back at approximately one hundred pounds. Obviously, he was unable to break his falls with his hands. Pathologists, examining the image, have identified damage to the knees and face suggesting one or more falls confirming tradition in the Way of the Cross. The *Bible* reference to Simon of Cyrene, being pressed to help him, speaks further to the weakened condition of this otherwise mighty man.

Meditation:

Oh, Jesus, if only man would learn; but, using his great gift of free will and with eyes, that are not your eyes which see eternity, but are short-sighted eyes that see through lenses clouded by the allurements of this world, allurements created not by God but by man, lies that have led us to worship the gifts of God as God Himself; so easily, we are led astray. So easily, we believe the lies when the true road to bliss is the narrow road of surrender to the will of the Father, as you surrendered, not to appease the Father's wrath against man, but to confirm the truth you taught and lived, a life of unselfish love. Thank you, Jesus, for loving me, for suffering and dying for me, that I might know the truth.

Prayer:

Father, as You see Your son, our brother, staggering and falling under the weight of his implement of death, Your great heart must be breaking; yet, You know not anger, the invention of man, which is now being wrought against Jesus. The heavy, rough wood is rubbing on top of the scourge wounds on top of the sensitized, painful skin from sweating blood. It is too much for clear eyes to behold; yet, rather than condemn, You pity the torturers and executioners; and Your great heart breaks for not only Your son but also for his executioners who are also Your beloved children. Thank You, Father, for so loving us. Amen.

Nail Wounds:

Blood flow can be seen at the left wrist (Page 102, front image) and at the feet (both body images) depicting nail wounds. Only the backs of the hands are visible. It is possible, based on latest information presented at the Shroud of Turin Conference in Richmond, Virginia, in June, 1999, that the entry point of the nail at the front of each hand was closer to the palm and the exit point at the back of the hand at the wrist. Damage to the median nerve would have caused the thumb to contract and not be visible on the image. Also pathologists have concluded from the image that one nail was used to affix both feet to the cross. The primary cause of death from crucifixion was asphyxiation. The victim found breathing extremely difficult while hanging from his arms. He would have to push his body up from the nailed feet; but the pain was so severe he would again drop until, again, suffocating, he would, again, push up. Some victims would thus labor and linger for days.

Meditation:

Jesus, we can see your strong body. Why did you die after only six agonizing hours on the cross? The trauma and blood loss, the night before, certainly weakened you. The scourging, known as the "half death," after hematidrosis, was even more painful than we can imagine. And the crown of thorns, it would seem, was inflicted by people who were determined that you would know no rest from new and more horrible pain and humiliation. Now the nails! Pounded again and again through your flesh and into the wood, the ultimate imprisonment, nailed, no escape possible now. How is it possible for man to be so cruel to man, even today, as innocent babies are destroyed in the womb, even today, as the elderly are cast aside by the very ones they gave their lives to, even today, as we execute our criminals instead of giving them the love they never had, the love you taught us to give? Why is this? Is it all for convenience? Is it all to preserve the evil ways of a stubborn race, bent on its own destruction? Some say, Jesus, that you died from a broken heart, from the sadness and heartbreak at the evil evolution of the creatures who were created to be friends of the Father.

Prayer:

"Father, forgive them for they know not what they do." Thank You, Father, for forgiving them and for forgiving me; for I too am guilty of crucifying Your son, every time I go against his teaching of loving all others, every time I ignore a hand reaching to me for help, every time I let my priorities stand in the way of my obedience to You. Thank You, Father, and please give me strength to do Your will and wisdom to know I can do nothing without You. Amen.

Spear Wound:

Adjacent to a triangular patch (page 102), covering fire damage which occurred in 1532, and below the right breast a bright area can be seen showing the result of the spear thrust into the side of Jesus. Pathologists have confirmed, as the Gospels indicate, that Jesus was already dead at the time of this wound. By the character of the blood stains they determined also that his heart was pierced by the spear; but, because of separation of the blood components, that the heart had already stopped beating; and the cause of death was either asphyxiation or cardiac and respiratory arrest. Though differing in opinions of cause of death, all professional examiners agreed that the man of the Shroud was indeed dead.

Meditation:

The final wound given your beleaguered body is a spear thrust which you cannot feel. At last, Jesus, your body is without pain. The thrust is skillfully given for it pierces your broken heart and the soldier is satisfied that you are dead. Had he doubted, your legs would have been broken, as with the others crucified with you, to hasten death before the approaching Sabbath. Little did he know his important role, not as one of your persecutors, but for the evidence he would produce that millennia later would scientifically confirm that Jesus of Nazareth did indeed die on his cross. Your soul, Jesus, departed its battered, grotesque envelope of flesh and, as you promised, with the soul of the one known as the good thief, "this day," entered paradise.

Prayer:

Father, Your son has completed his mission on earth and now returns to You, not as the prodigal son, but as the faithful son who taught Your truth and lived Your truth to the shedding of his last drop of blood and breathing his last breath. He returns to You victorious in demonstrating Your way and Your truth and the New Birth to life in You. Two thousand years later, Father, as we are poised upon a new millennium, people are still ignoring Your message through Jesus; but he continues to teach; and more are enlightened and reborn; and so it will continue until, through him, You have remade the earth into a new heaven on earth; and Your glory reigns from sea to sea. Then, Father, the truth will be known throughout the earth and Your people will be truly free. Amen.

The Face of Jesus of Nazareth

on

The Holy Shroud of Turin

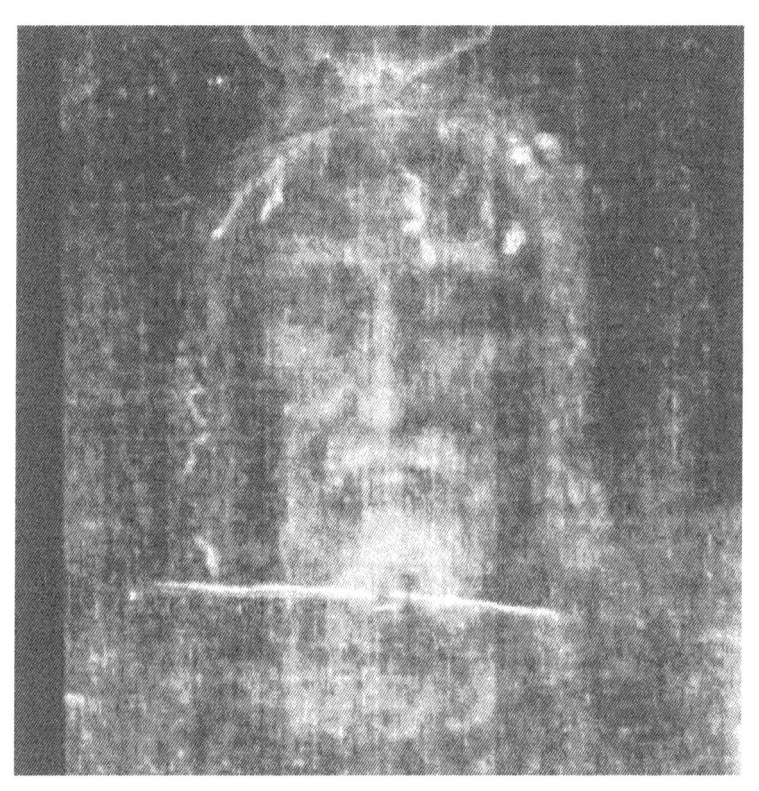

FACE OF JESUS OF NAZARETH
AS VIEWED ON
PHOTOGRAPHIC NEGATIVE IMAGE
OF
THE SHROUD OF TURIN

The Holy Shroud of Turin

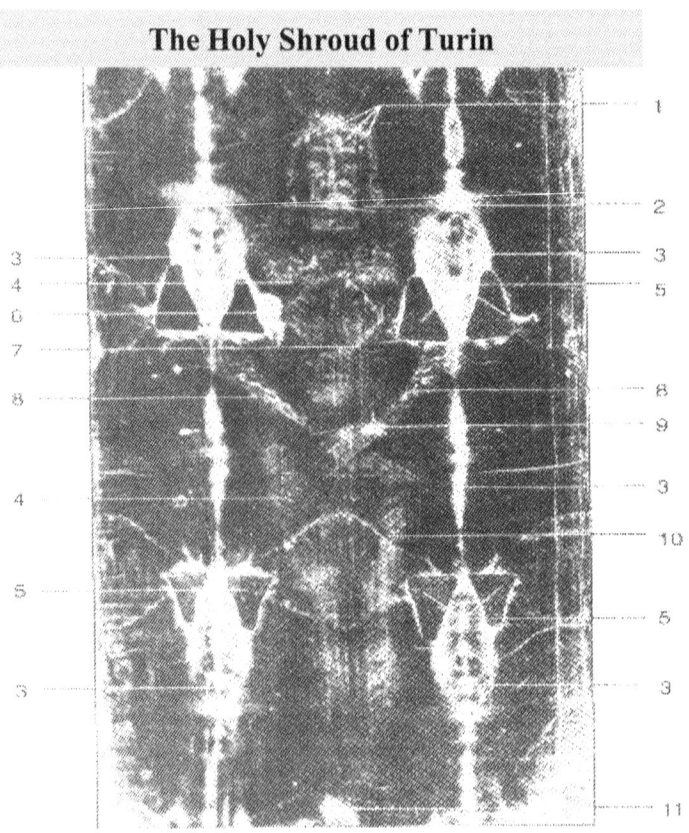

The Holy Shroud of Turin

Front Image

1. Crown of thorn wounds; **2**. *Crease in linen*; **3**. *Burns from 1532 fire*; **4**. *Scourge marks*; **5**. *Repair from fire*; **6**. *Side wound from Spear*; **7**. *Water marks (from the fire)*; **8**. *Blood flow on arms*; **9**. *Nail wounds*; **10**. *Water marks (from the fire)*; **11**. *Nail wounds in feet*

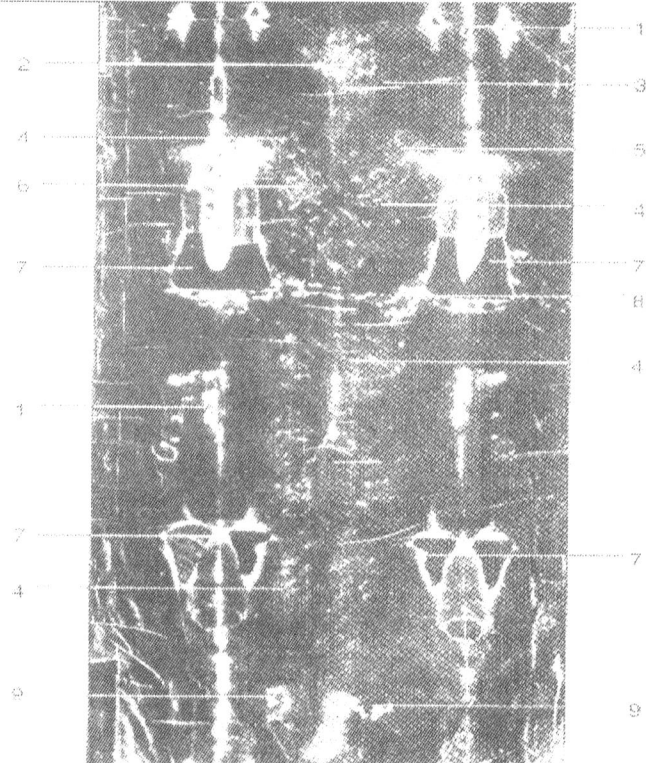

Back Image

1. *Burns*; **2**. *Crown of thorn wounds*; **3**. *Crease in linen*; **4**. *Scourge marks*; **5**. *Shoulder wound*; **6**. *Left shoulder-blade wound*; **7**. *Repair from fire*; **8**. *Blood flow from side wound*; **9**. *Nail wound*

--Images Courtesy of Russ Breault, Founder of the Shroud of Turin Education Project, Inc.
(http://www.shroud2000.com)

The Blood of Jesus

Pathologists were also able to determine from the unsmeared blood stains, that the cloth was not lifted from Jesus' body, either by himself or anyone else; therefore, since the cloth was still in the tomb, according to the Gospels, when viewed by the Apostles, we must assume no one had removed the body from the Shroud or the tomb. The character of bloodstains would indicate, based on the scientific investigation of 1978, that the body dematerialized while in the cloth. This is in accord with Einstein's theory that matter and energy are interconvertible. Indeed this writer would speculate that the very action or power which created the image caused the body to dematerialize. I believe that power to be the One, who the *Bible* credits with raising Jesus from the dead, Almighty God Himself. Exactly when Jesus' spirit body and soul separated from his corpse we can't be sure; but, according to the *Bible* he proclaimed to the good thief, "This day you will be with me in paradise," certainly good news for all of us.

Also, in reference to the bloodstains, a new book on the Shroud, *The DNA of God?*, presents that the analysis of the ancient blood taken from the shroud shows the full complement of forty-six chromosomes, twenty-three from the mother and twenty-three from the human father including the Y Chromosome, pointing toward Jesus being fully human and not conceived without a human father, unless we are to believe that the Holy Spirit, which the *Bible* depicts as the only father of Jesus, provided the necessary human factors. The author, who is apparently a devout Catholic, answers the question of his title not with science, which is the basis of the remainder of his presentation, but with reference to the four councils of the early church from 325 to 451 which proclaimed Jesus as God and equal to the Father. Thus, he concludes that the DNA of the Shroud is the DNA of God.

I believe his conclusion to be so weak, based on the proclamations not of God or Jesus but mere men, that the author's scientific examination and scientific results provide overwhelming evidence that the man of the Shroud of Turin, was not virgin born and was not Deity, but was a fully, normal human male. While he gives some evidence of virgin conceptions of embryonic tumors, he gives no evidence of such tumors becoming living children much less male children. I have further come to believe, even though Pope John Paul II has referred to the Shroud as a true relic, the reason for the Catholic Church not making an official proclamation of what has become so obvious to so many in the scientific community, that it is indeed the true burial cloth of Jesus of Nazareth, is there exists among the hierarchy of the Church a concern, or even fear, that this most unique, most revealing, most authentic of relics could be used to dispute the deity of Jesus.

Not only does this not diminish Jesus in my eyes; but it enhances what he did as a fellow human being out of his love for his Father, for the truth, which he was and is, and his love for you and me. Perhaps this is one reason we, as humans, have had so much trouble in living by his words and example because we saw them coming from something more than mere man. And, thus, now at last, we can be freed from the myth, from man's concoction of God literally in human form. Now, in seeing Jesus, as he really was and is, a man indeed with a special purpose, a man who totally surrendered to God's will, a man with God living in and through him. We can allow the truth to set us free because we can live by his words and example, if we will but follow his example of trust and surrender. He was and is one of us, nothing more, nothing less; and He told us such over and over again. "Greater works than these will you do." True, he is immortal, divine, of the essence of the Father, which he taught is also ours for the asking. Praise God!

My true brother, Jesus, I love you for bringing God's freedom to my soul. No longer will I dishonor you by worshipping you as God. Humankind unjustly nailed you to the cross and humankind has also unjustly nailed deity to you. Thank you for teaching the truth both through the Bible and through James Padgett and most especially through your Holy Shroud of Turin. Now we can see why the Father produced this wonderful relic, this pictorial gospel of your passion, the price you paid to bring us the truth. He knew, by man's history, that man would proclaim you God. Your silent witness has waited two thousand years for humankind to be ready to receive the truth, proclaimed by your burial linen, that you are the human son of the Father who has come to lead us home. Thank you, my true brother, Jesus. Amen.

The Risen Body

We can assume from the *Bible* that the body Jesus occupied after the tomb was different from his crucified, grotesque body. His risen body needed no recovery time to perform normally and beyond normality; and no reference is made anywhere, that it was grotesque to view, which obviously was true of the body in the Shroud. He was not easily identified by those who had been close to him; yet his risen body retained the wounds from the nails and spear.

We, therefore, present that Jesus' crucified body was not raised from the dead but experienced a form of rapid or accelerated decomposition or dematerialization or conversion from matter to energy, forming the unique image of the unique man, truly the Christ sent from God; for we know of no such comparable incident with visual record claimed for any other human being or purported man-god in all of history. The Shroud of Turin, in the opinion of this writer, is the silent witness to one of the greatest occurrences in human history, preserved against all odds, as the one sign that Jesus said would be given, the sign of Jonah, the man himself, in this instance Jesus himself, or all that materially remained of his crucified body, the image and the blood.

This would also help to explain how Jesus could suddenly appear with the Apostles in a locked room or how he could suddenly disappear from the presence of the two disciples he, according to the *Bible* "in a different form," met on the road to Emmaus. Yet, we have reason to believe he was not a ghost, as in the former example, Thomas examined his wounds and in the latter he broke bread. Spirit materialization or control of physical elements has been experienced or witnessed by many people including myself.

106

In 1997, I was in my car stopped at a traffic light at a busy intersection in the left turn lane when my engine quit. It would not restart; so I turned on my emergency flashers, got out, opened the hood, and started for a service station at the corner close by. As I reached the sidewalk, I was approached by a trio consisting of a man, a woman, and a pre-teen boy who inquired about my problem. Continuing my pace and direction, I explained I was about to call my towing service. They immediately expressed their desire to help by pushing the car through the intersection. Surprised and appreciative, I climbed behind the wheel and they pushed. Reaching the curb safely, I was about to exit when they insisted on pushing me to a nearby shopping center parking lot where the car would be safely off the road; and they did so with surprising ease.

Secure in a parking space, I exited my car with the thought of treating this nice family to dinner, since it was late in the day; but no one was there. There were no obstructions to my line of sight. I had not lingered in the car. But they had vanished seemingly into thin air. I called the towing service and, while waiting, thankfully pondered this experience. This incident has contributed to my subsequent study of and belief in the angelic realm. We indeed are not alone.

Inspired writers have convinced me that every person on earth has a minimum of two guardian angels. They have also convinced me that angels, which we think of as separate creations of God, are actually people who have left the envelope of flesh, have crossed over to the spirit world as we all do, and are continuing to serve God and man.

On the day of his physical death, Jesus, accompanied by the good thief, crossed over to the spirit world and announced throughout, from the highest heavens to the lowest hells, that God had restored to all humankind, both on earth and in the spirit spheres, the potential to receive His Divine Essence and become one with Him. And, as he related to the disciples, he has established and continues to prepare the higher Celestial Heavens for those who seek and receive this greatest of all of God's gifts to His children, His very essence, His Divine Love.

Jesus was the first to enter this state of being and place where only those, who have sought, have found.

As a final comment on the suffering passion of Jesus, this writer believes that, though God did not cause or instigate this injustice, He did allow it; thereby showing us, when we unjustly accuse Him as the source of tragedies in our lives, He does allow them to happen but always for good purpose. If we focus on the tragedy rather than on God and the discerning of His purpose, we commit a great error. Perhaps the worst tragedy one can experience is the loss or suffering of a loved one. If we truly believe the deceased go to a better place, while it's okay to experience personal loss and even grieve for a short time, we should rejoice at the victory experienced at being freed from the envelope of flesh and all its limitations. How can we be other than happy for the deceased unless we fear they go to eternal damnation, which is another total myth and concoction of man, which we will later discuss?

More important than Jesus suffering passion was his mission that led to it, his divine passion, his passion of great desire, which was to fulfill his Father's will on earth. Every one of us is given a divine purpose which, if we heed its call, can become our divine passion. Oh, it may not be to change the world. It may involve loving only one other person; but, perhaps, that person's given purpose is to change the world; therefore, we play our part in the will of God which is the only important thing.

Think about this for just a minute. What is there that can be so important in the achievements of a single life on earth that can compare to doing the will of our Creator Father to Whom we return. The Gospels make many references to an accounting where those, who are given much, are expected to multiply the gifts they are given not for themselves but for others and for God. The significance of the story of the mother of Jesus in the *Bible*, be it truth or myth, is to illustrate the ripple effect that one "yes" can have when that "yes" is to God.

How can one discern his or her divine purpose? The single most important answer to that question for me has been

SURRENDER. When we surrender to God, it is the opposite of surrendering to man. When we surrender to man, we are surrendering at least a part of our freedom. This is easiest to see in marriage or our jobs. I am not saying this is wrong; it is indeed a part of our life on earth and with that life comes relationships with others and with those relationships come obligations.

It is when our earthly obligations are given priority over serving God that we get into trouble. So surrendering to God, doesn't mean we stop functioning in the world. It means we function better in the world and with others even, if for a time, we seem to become out of sync with them. As Jesus defined, our one great duty to others, as well as to God, is to love. He also told us to seek and we will find; and, to me, the most important way to seek our God given purpose is to surrender to Him; for, when we discover it and say yes to it, we say yes to freedom and everything that goes with it including, ultimately, oneness with Him where His will becomes our will.

As Jesus grew from boyhood to manhood in Egypt and Galilee, he studied and prayed and surrendered to God and discovered his divine purpose; and it became his passion of great desire; it became his life; and, I believe, his dedication to fulfilling that purpose has created more good and more good works in the world than the fulfilled passion of any other single person to have walked this earth. This is his living testament to the truth he taught and lived; and that truth was love, love of God, love of neighbor, love of enemy, and love of self. And the greatest expression of love of self is total surrender to the will of God.

Without this surrender we cannot be reborn; and we seek rebirth not for its rewards but because it is the will of God, going all the way back to the beginning of the *Bible* and, I would suspect, of most texts considered holy by the great religions of the world, where He created us not to be objects of manipulation or punishment but of His great love, seeking friendship, freely returned, from us through our obedience, our love, and our surrender. Without this surrender to the will of God, we cannot really forgive which, I believe, is the toughest aspect of love. We simply can't do it without God's help; yet, do it we must; for, if we seek oneness with Him, there can be no unforgiveness in our hearts as there is none in His. And what greater demonstration of forgiveness, through surrender, than Jesus.

He taught us how to love and how to be born again. This was both his passion and his divine purpose. Above everything else, he was a messenger and a teacher. His healing of people and his suffering simply supported that purpose but were ancillary to it. Though his passion, his legacy, his teaching, has greatly blessed the world and, perhaps, even prevented its self destruction, its greatest benefit to humankind is not of this world but the next where each of us spends eternity.

Thank you, Jesus, for surrendering and for selflessly caring. Amen.

V. THE FATHER'S LOVE

God of Love

"God is love" is the theme or the common thread which runs all through the New Testament. It is an advancement in man's perception of the Almighty from the warrior god or the wrathful god of the Old Testament to the Benevolent God of the New, though we can see the love aspect in the Old, moreso in the Psalms.

When I wrote *40 Days to Freedom*, the Spirit of God directed that I use excerpts from Psalms for the daily readings. This was the only possible cause for such direction as I was even more a New Testament, Four Gospels Christian then than now. However, the leading was never questioned. I obeyed; and I fell in love with the Psalms as I studied them for the first time with my new eyes. And I saw that He chose the Psalms because He is the God of love. This would also later serve me as a validation of the Padgett Messages.

So often, God will lead us in a certain direction without explaining why. He wants us to follow His lead in faith and trust that His intent is only the best for us and our project or purpose in life, whatever it may be. Well, you may ask, how can I be sure that a leading is of God? The answer is always LOVE. He will always lead us in the way of love. I believe there will usually also be a spiritual experience with God's direction. It may be a feeling or a knowing or the inner voice or a vision.

Second Rebirth

At the end of 1997, through my inner voice, God told me I was to experience another kind of rebirth, different from when I had received the eyes of Jesus in 1990. He told me I would learn to be dependent on Him alone for everything, including my financial needs. I suddenly realized why my fund-raising efforts of the past two years had failed as He had told me at the beginning of '96 to "Distribute the books and I'll take care of the rest." I had not realized how literally He meant this very powerful message but was now aware my attempts at fund-raising were simply an extension of my self-dependence of my previous twenty-eight years in the money business.

To this new revelation my audible answer was "WOW!" My Father's immediate return was, "At least I did not require you sacrifice a son or daughter;" and I knew He was referring to the story of Abraham and Isaac in Genesis to indicate that my sacrifice of material wealth would be relatively small. This dialogue occurred in the early morning darkness as I was riding my bicycle which is usually a time of prayer and meditation.

When I returned home, I quickly went to Genesis and at the end of this part of the Abraham story, God told Abraham, "Your descendants will be as numerous as the stars in the sky and the grains of sand on the seashore." And He told me, "So too, will be your descendants who are not your physical descendants but those who are freed through the message of *40 Days to Freedom*." Then I read, "And your descendants will defeat their enemies." And He said, "So too will your descendants defeat their enemies of addiction and harmful obsession and habitual sin." And finally I read, "All peoples will want the same blessings of your descendants" which confirmed a second powerful message from the beginning of '96 that "This message will blanket the earth," referring to the message of *40 Days to Freedom* and *The Man in the Desert*.

As a side note, as mentioned earlier, God called Freedom Ministries, Inc. into full-time service with a trilogy of short powerful messages of which I have just related two. The third was, "The organized churches are filled with addicts who are not receiving what they need to break their chains of addiction," referring to not only substance abuse but all habitual sin as we also have earlier presented.

Soon after the powerful revelation of second rebirth, my savings were exhausted on ministry expenses; and I could no longer continue Peggy's salary. I had kept her informed of what was happening; and she stayed aboard as long as possible but finally had to leave my employment.

Next, I was not able to pay rent for my office and my condo and believed that God wanted me to give up the office. Then I had a vision of my pet cat, Ucf, sitting on my lap on the couch in my office and knew it was the condo which had to go and I was to move my home to my office. I applied my condo security deposit to cover the rent I owed and made the move which primarily meant moving Ucf. This was a concern since he has epilepsy and has a tendency toward seizures when moved from his normal environment. I would even have to tranquilize him for his annual visits to the vet; but I decided not to for this very short move and left him in God's hands.

To my relief, he exited his carrier in his new home, explored the three hundred fifty square feet and settled right in. The vision is now fulfilled, every morning, as he is on my lap on the office couch, when I'm in study and meditation. It's our favorite time of each day; and, though changes to my lifestyle were necessary, I've never been happier. This is just the normal result for anyone being obedient to the Father and pursuing his life's purpose.

By May 8, 1998, we were two months behind on office rent and telephone; and I owed taxes I couldn't pay. It strangely seemed I had recently heard, many times in my television Christian study, that God is never late with his provision. Before falling behind with my obligation one televangelist said, "Sometimes He's just in the nick of time;" and I said, "Thank you, God. I know that was for me." As I started falling behind, I started trying to think of other ways to raise money and I heard, "I thought you were standing." I responded, "Yes, Lord" and resolved I would continue to stand in faith in God's provision alone, no matter what! This was it! I experienced a lightness of spirit and a wonderful peace that I was in my Father's hands. I gave away my last dollar with a smile on my face and in my heart and then, May eighth.

I was working on the computer in my outer office about noontime; and there was a knock at the door which I opened. A lady with a German accent entered extending her hand and expressing that she was pleased to meet me. Now, I had never met nor talked with this woman before; but she was clutching a copy of *40 Days to Freedom*; and, pointing to it said excitedly,

"This is the answer! This is the answer!" We didn't have long to share, as I was scheduled for jail ministry, but enough that I learned that she too had a powerful story of God's saving power. She convinced me she should take a case of books for her friends; and I carried them to her car.

About three hours later, I returned to my office and resumed my work that had been so blessedly interrupted and noticed a piece of multi-folded paper on the desk that had not been there before. As I unfolded it, I discovered a check for one thousand dollars! Later that same day two more significant checks arrived in the mail from prison ministry brothers who had never before contributed; but both later confessed a strong moving to do so at that time. Also, the lady later shared that she had a strong compelling, that morning, that she must meet the author of her newly treasured book, not knowing why or intending to contribute.

By the end of May 8, 1998, my office rent and telephone were brought current and owed taxes paid with forty-two dollars remaining. I had learned that I literally can depend on God for all my needs; and that, while we are being tested, He welcomes our testing Him in this regard, which is also Biblical. I had also learned that God's definition of "on time" and ours may be quite different. By the way, with my late office rent, I owed two months penalties which I was not required to pay. Our God is certainly an awesome God!

Now, about a year and a half later, I can truthfully say I have not known a financial crunch since this wonderful second rebirthing. I have no concern for livelihood, as that is in my Father's hands; and, though materially poor, I am free to spend all my time in His direction and endeavors. Even now, as I write, with no publishing connections and no money to self-publish this work, I can see Him opening doors.

God Dependence

The point I'm hoping to make, with the sharing of my second rebirth, is that I feel as I must be the most blessed, most free person on earth; but I could not experience this without the trials He's guided me through. Now, God has not caused me any

114

discomfort or displeasure. Those I have caused myself, both in my addiction and in my self-dependence, losing sight that I cannot draw my next breath without the love of my eternal Father.

Rather than causing my problems, He orchestrated my freedom from them; and, yes, He will allow me to experience more challenges; but, as I have learned, I always grow, soul and spirit, through His overcoming; and I can, therefore, now welcome the trials. And, strange as it may seem, I can even thank Him for allowing the forty year addiction. He will allow us to stumble and fall, many times, if we persist in our own strength. But, each time, He offers His freedom; and, through rebirth in His Divine Love, our opportunity for service and joy is greater as the recovery is greater.

I use the word "orchestrate" to describe God's work with us because He has taught me He refuses to manipulate, to invade the free will of man. Rather than manipulate, His way is gentle persuasion, always giving us a choice, sometimes gently persuading others in our behalf as demonstrated in my story of second rebirth. I can almost see Him, like a conductor before a huge symphony orchestra, with His hands raised in gentle, flowing, never abrupt movement, conducting the harmonious melody and movement of the universe. How awesome He is!

Of course, this is not an accurate vision of God; but it is one that He allows me to have as His precious child. Indeed, I have grown in His love to the extent I often feel as if I am His only child; and, all my Father has to do, all day, every day, is love me. Thank you, Father! Of course, I am not His only child, any more than Jesus is; but He loves me as much as Jesus and as much as the worst sinner who has ever walked this earth.

We Are Soul

In Padgett, Jesus tells us that God is Soul, without physical body and without spirit body, as He has no need for either. Certainly, a demonstration of His love for His highest creation is that we are truly made in His image as we too are each soul created by Him. Our souls then seek incarnation in the physical bodies prepared by our biological parents and are at the same time incarnated in our spirit bodies.

So it has been for every person on earth since our original parents; and there have been no virgin births which are strictly the creation of the mind of man. Also, there is none of the substance of God in us until we are born again; and we are given firm evidence which, I believe, could be considered scientific, in our transformation. We become new creatures, new creations, though the same people. In fact, I was amazed that the transformation, that so radically changed my thoughts and my behavior, left my individuality intact. In other words, I was still me.

I point this out since, I believe, many feel reluctant to become religious or turn to God because they feel the transformation may rob them of their identity, as unique individuals, and fear becoming, as sometimes depicted in media as religious robots. Just the opposite is true. When we are without God we are robots. We may feel we are strong, self-reliant individuals, but this is a mask we're wearing and a lie we're both buying and selling; for, in truth, we can do nothing without Him. Of course, this is something most of us have to experience; and, credit to the mystery of God's ways, the deeper the fall away from Him, again, the more glorious and powerful the recovery.

I used to feel sad for those never tested in the pit but have come to realize we all are tested, even the saints; and, usually, they even more. Those, whom we perceive as not tested, are perhaps tested in different ways from ourselves. Sometimes, and I believe often, they are not aware of the test themselves, other than a knowledge that their lives are not as happy as they should be. They often wear a facade of happiness and success, which is not surprising since we live in a society that encourages such facades, by directing us to all the false gods of materialism and pride and sex and power and over-indulgence and even religion.

True Freedom

There is only one healthy obsession which happens to also be the only true Source of lasting joy and peace. He is the only

One who will never imprison us. He is also the only Source of true freedom which He will never attempt to steal from us. Science will tell us to replace a bad habit with a good one. This is why the procedure of *40 Days to Freedom* will overcome any addiction. The good habit is God through spiritual rebirth, receiving His Divine Love which, in addition to being His essence, is the greatest power in the universe. And, when we have the greatest power living within us, when properly applied, nothing can withstand it. It becomes the way, the truth, and the life that was and is Jesus; and, as he proclaimed, when we apply it in faith, it will set us free. As a matter of fact, faith grows immeasurably with receiving Divine Love. If we have not this Essence of God, we are not likely to have strong faith.

Yet, our Father loves us so much and takes such care to not trample our freedom that our free will remains intact. So, it is possible for one reborn to backslide, to doubt, and to even go astray. At a conference I attended a couple years ago, during his presentation, a prison minister testified about a revelation he had received from God, that once a person is reborn, the flame of the Holy Spirit, which I have identified as the Divine Love of God, can never be extinguished. He spoke of this as if it was the greatest revelation in the life of this man senior to me in years and, probably, experience with God at the time.

By coincidence, I later received the same message from Jesus in Padgett that once received, by the human soul, the Divine Love can never be replaced. When we backslide, it may seem dormant; but it remains, waiting to be reignited. The prison minister applied his revelation and started polling groups of prisoners and found, in every audience that the majority were backsliders. He realized, if he changed his message to minister to those people instead of to non-Christians, he could multiply his efforts on the prison compounds by, instead of creating new Christians, creating new Christian ministers.

Coincidence?

I have experienced so many like coincidences in my walk with God. I have come to realize there are no coincidences; and this is not my revelation alone since, by coincidence, I have recently discovered that the perception of meaningful coincidence has been given a name, synchronicity. According to Doctor Carl Jung, this is a law in the universe which causes humans to grow in consciousness. I would hazard an addition to this assertion that synchronicity is the realization of God's orchestration of the universe and our lives for good purpose; and His greatest purpose is His friendship with man, which blossoms into full fruition, when we experience our final transformation into the Divine Angel, the ultimate expression of sonship with God.

This is the message of Jesus. This was his good habit, which he was compelled to pass on no matter what the cost; and, as we know, he paid the ultimate price. And God loves us so much, not only did He allow Jesus to pay the price, realizing the penalty was fleeting in comparison to an eternity of blissful sonship, but He also gave us a rare human glimpse at the supernatural, or some may say the accelerated natural, in the form of a pictorial record or gospel of Jesus' expression of the way, the truth, and the life, which is love. It's all about love!

Faith and Reason

Religion teaches a network of paradoxes about the love of God. First they want us to believe that He is love; yet, that He also expresses wrath and anger, which some try to explain as a part of His love; or others say we can't understand but must accept in faith. Granted, we cannot understand everything about God and that's fine, as we are not God and never will be. But God is not unreasonable; and He does not contradict Himself; nor does He break His own laws. Religion would have us believe He told us not to kill; but, that He has willfully destroyed societies such as Sodom and Gomorrah. No, there is a true message in that story; but it is not about the wrath of God, it is about the self-imposed consequence of the evil created by man. According to Jesus in Padgett, if we are a member of an evil society, though we ourselves are good, if we remain associated with that society, we will reap what it sows.

We are told by religion that God is jealous; and, also, that He told us not to covet. We are told in heaven there is no sin,

118

which I believe is true of the Celestial Heavens; yet we are to believe that the most glorious of angels sinned and became the devil, the orchestrater of all evil. It is time for the truth to be exposed and for Christianity to stop burying its head in the sand of myth; for the truth is far more glorious than the myth and paradoxes can ever hope to be. The truth is simple and easy to understand and rooted in John's statement that "God is love."

Anything contrary to love is contrary to God. Anything of love is of God. Nothing contrary to love was created by God as He does not create disharmony. All that is contrary to love was created by man, as man is the only creator, aside from God, in the universe. Religion has created ambiguity and distrust of God, when He is the only one who is trustworthy; and I would include God through Jesus, as trustworthy, with the caveat that I believe Jesus' representations in the Padgett Messages, of the twentieth century, to be more accurate and trustworthy than those in the *Bible*, of the first and second centuries, as they were less subject to human errors through translation and misunderstanding and method of transmission. I should also add that the two sources are in accord in His overall message of love. It's all about love!

The Future of Organized Religion

What does this say about the future of religion in America and in the world? I believe that religious traditions, that remain stubbornly rooted in myth and paradox, as God increasingly reveals His truth to humankind, will fall by the wayside. According to Jesus in Padgett, their ministers and teachers and members, who remain steadfast in their ways of error, will carry their stubborn ways into the spirit world where they will know darkness before coming into the light. And the ministers and teachers who have led others astray will know more and longer, self-imposed torment when they see the bad fruit of their labor.

These penalties are not imposed by the loving Father, any more than He imposed the cross on Jesus, but by their own disharmony and divorce from the truth. Indeed, as Jesus in Padgett reveals, if they were immediately allowed to the Celestial Heavens, they would experience even greater suffering from their disharmony than from their gradual path out of darkness into light.

But the light of God's truth and harmony will eventually be known and experienced by all either in the heavens of the spirit world or the heavens of the divine, which is the will of God, as expressed in the *Bible* by Jesus. This is in accord with the God of Love. You see, there is no unforgiveness in God, again, according to Jesus in Padgett. Religion tells us, through Jesus in the *Bible*, that we must forgive all; yet, also tells us that God harbors unforgiveness against His children. Not only does He forgive us, but He forgives through us; otherwise, how else is it possible for a parent to forgive the murderer of her child, as I and many others have witnessed? To me, such forgiveness is not possible for man operating on his own apart from God. It is only possible if man allows God to live and work through him. When we pray, "Forgive us our trespasses as we forgive those who trespass against us," we, in truth, are asking the impossible unless we surrender and allow Him to forgive through us.

Again, we are faced with the easy way or the hard way. Either we struggle and try to do right, even live by the Ten Commandments; or, we allow Him to flow, His love to flow through us. He never refuses to forgive us, even if we don't ask, even if we don't forgive others; but, when we don't, then we are held in unforgiveness, not by God but by ourselves. Jesus in the *Bible* says, "Whose sins you forgive, they are forgiven; and, whose sins you retain, they are retained." Retained by who? Not by God; but by you! This is why unforgiving people lead such miserable lives, every one of them. If there was any unforgiveness in God, those unforgiving would be in harmony with God and would be happy, not miserable.

But what about where Jesus said, "If you do not forgive, don't expect your Heavenly Father to forgive you?" Perhaps, he said simply, "don't expect to be forgiven." which could easily mean forgiven by yourself. If the former is more accurate, he isn't saying that God holds in unforgiveness but may be referring to God allowing you to hold yourself in unforgiveness which is also compatible with the latter. As angry people are generally angry at themselves, so too, I believe unforgiving people are unforgiving of themselves.

The sin of unforgiveness, as all sin, carries its own penalty. God pities us rather than condemns us; and, as the father in the Parable of the Prodigal Son, Father God stands forever watching and eager for our return with open arms of love, not of condemnation or unforgiveness. I believe it's possible, the truth of Jesus was more accurately preserved in his parables, than in some of his other teachings written in the *Bible*, as these stories would less lend themselves to manipulation by man.

Those religions and denominations, that grow in the love and truth of God, and evolve away from the myth and error of man, I believe, will grow and prosper. All religions need to focus less on ceremonies of worship and focus more on freeing members from bondage to habitual sin. Thus, in doing the will of God and Jesus in "freeing the captives," a religion or church is "worshipping in spirit and in truth." Creation of a new religion is not necessary but the evolution of the existing ones is, if they are to survive, as man will continue in his enlightenment about God and himself with or without them.

I have hope for my denomination and others, as well, and other love-centered religions. But, I fear, that for some change may come too slowly for their survival, as more enlightenment comes from sources without, rather than within organized religion. This was true with Jesus who though a Jew was seen as operating and teaching outside of the religious boundaries of his day. Similar statements could be made about James Padgett, a Methodist, and this writer, a Roman Catholic, and I would suspect those of other substantial religions, who have shared their seemingly radical revelations of truth with the world.

Spirit

There is, today, a movement underway, in my church and others, with more focus on spiritual rebirth through the Holy Spirit. The people involved would be especially blessed by study of the Padgett Messages (www.divine.org) as they would learn, that in the process of being "born again," that they are receiving the Divine Love of the Father through the Holy Spirit;

121

and, that rather than one of three person in a triune God, the Holy Spirit is a special instrument or expression of the monotheistic Father God. Further, the Holy Spirit is a part of the Spirit of God which is omnipresent throughout the universe.

The function of the Holy Spirit is specialized to only being the instrument of deliverance of the Divine Love Essence of God to the human soul who has expressed heart-felt, sincere desire. The Spirit of God is responsible for all of the other functions and operations of God expressed throughout the universe including grooming and nourishing humankind in knowledge and awareness of God and helping me write this book.

God is Soul, without spirit body or physical body; and His Spirit is the active energy of His Soul. Likewise man is soul; and the active energy of man's soul is his spirit. This is how man is created in the image only of God, as we have discusssed; and man is not divine or immortal until he is born again, though he may live forever at the discretion of God. But, when born again and ultimately transformed into the Divine Angel, man then has absolute knowledge of his immortality. Without this final transformation, which I would associate with the Transfiguration of Jesus, man may think or speculate or believe he is immortal; but he is not until he has the knowledge of the Divine Angel who is one in mind and will and love with God.

By the way, there is speculation that all the events of the Gospels did not happen in the chronological order written, including the Transfiguration of Jesus, which, now more than ever, I believe was a real event. Again, I believe every event or story in the *Bible* has significance and has an important truth to teach to humankind, as I also believe that God allows nothing to happen without purpose, whether it is His creation or orchestration or man's.

I am currently reading the latest work of author James Redfield entitled The Celestine Vision. I believe it could also be called his Celestial Vision as I am enjoying and learning from it, immensely. He refers to humans competing through various means to draw energy from each other; and, I guess, we could substitute, based on what we have just shared, spirit for the word energy. James relates that in these one-on-one confrontations, such as intimidation, there is always a winner who gains energy or spirit and a loser who loses. As I read this, God's Spirit spoke to me that, when we draw our energy from God, we no longer need to take energy from others; and, in fact, can freely give our / His energy to others, resulting in our always being replenished with God's energy / Spirit. I believe this could qualify as another definition of agape love. In other words, love begets love; and, as givers, we can't outgive God.

When we take from others, and I believe James would agree with me by his examples given, we are victimizing. When we freely give to others, without thought of return, we are loving and being a blessing. When we graciously accept from others, we are allowing them to be a blessing as we are all blessed by the Father, His Spirit, His love, flowing through His children.

I read a few books at a time, including my own, as it is also an important source to me for learning about God. I will not share from all I am reading as I write; however, this seemed especially appropriate as it occurred during my work on this chapter about the Father's love. Certainly, the offering of His great Spirit to help us and groom us and teach us and, yes, even to energize us, is an awesome expression of His great love for every one of us.

God Doesn't Manipulate

Now some might respond, "What do you mean help and groom and teach and energize? I haven't seen or experienced any of that!" To which I must ask, have you sought? Jesus taught we must seek to find and knock before the door will be opened; otherwise, again, God would be violating our free will, which He is most careful not to do. Imagine, if you will, a god that truly would be angered. There are those who are saying we are seeing His wrath now, as predicted by Nostradamus and others, as we approach the new millennium. Floods, earthquakes, hurricanes, droughts, and other natural disasters are at an all-time high. Of course, Nostradamus didn't say these were expressions of God's wrath but many religious are so interpreting. They see these as warnings that man had better get his act together.

These natural events are just that. God doesn't manipulate nature any more than He manipulates man. You could say it is simply chance if you happen to experience one of these disasters; and, like the blessings of nature, the natural disasters fall on the good and the bad. This too is consistent with the *Bible*. And of those who are killed in the current disasters, if the unsaved, who had not claimed Jesus as savior, were consigned to the "eternal lake of fire," that would be the god of wrath; and the saved, who lost their lives, would also be seen as his victims.

God has no victims! He is love. Those affected by natural disasters are experiencing new challenges, new opportunities for growth closer to our Father, to make progress on our path back to Him. Those who die in the disasters are truly better off where they've gone if they haven't lived evil lives without repentance. If they have, those left behind are certainly better off without their influence. Those, who preach a wrathful god, deserve pity; for their impossible confusion they will never resolve until they see Him as all-loving. The belief that He is both love and wrath leads to stubborn dogmatism that casts a shadow on Christianity and attempts to win members through fear rather than love. This doesn't bring people closer to God, but, instead, forces submission to avoid damnation. This doesn't aid but impedes one's path to the Father and is the reason He sent Jesus.

Some come attracted by the love and then later become confused, when exposed to the false teaching of fear and wrath. Some buy into the premise that God so loved the world that He sacrificed His only son on the cross to appease His anger against humankind, or that the Father presented the son to be the sacrifice of humankind back to Him. These are actually preached as acts of a loving God. Jesus was accurate when he described such believers of the ridiculous of his day as well as this as "eyes that cannot see and ears that cannot hear." This would be comparable, in the Parable of the Wicked Tenants, to the landlord father sending his son to be killed by the tenant farmers to appease his anger for their having killed the servants he earlier sent. Most become confused by such false teaching resulting in people switching churches or stop attending services or just try to internally bury the conflict which was my reaction.

Christians and their teachers will never be at peace until they see that God is all-loving; and, in modern times as well as ancient times, that man is prone to error. Humankind received Jesus' message but, very soon after his departure, started manipulating it. Even so, some have seen the light, the message has survived; and he has returned to restate what was lost and modified through translation, misunderstanding, and intentional manipulation which, again, is allowed by God for purpose. Thank God, that in this age of information and discovery, we have also become more prone to the discovery of man's errors and less gullible to the unreasonable scenarios of modern-day Pharisees.

The Day of Judgment

Rather than display anger, the Father, again, sent the son; and, again, used an unlikely vessel, in the eyes of man, to receive His message of love and freedom. Again, due to the pattern of error and straying of man, the correction is needed, as two thousand years ago, for the misguided faithful as well as non-believers. The good news of Jesus, in his second coming through Padgett, is the New Heaven has arrived and the New Earth, heaven on earth, will also be realized. But man needs to not be complacent; and a sense of urgency is needed, especially for those who would seek oneness with the Father; for the Day of Judgment is true and, though we know not when, is coming.

On that day, the final chapter will be written on the divinity of man. Those who have not sought and received the Divine Love will no longer have the opportunity. The sheep will be separated from the goats; the born again from the unsaved. The sheep will reside in the Celestial Heavens, the New Heaven; and the goats will all, eventually, enjoy the heaven of the spirit world. The sheep will have absolute knowledge of their own immortality; and the goats will not.

The New Earth will likewise have its heavenly realm and the disharmony of sin will no longer exist. This is the plan of the all-loving Father God as revealed by Jesus two thousand years ago and, again, in the early years of this twentieth century. The ball, so to speak, is now in man's court. What a glorious opportunity! What an awesome God!

VI. In the Presence

Free at Last

After my healing in 1990, I was free to do anything I wanted. Can you imagine a person, who had been in bondage to the sin of lust all his life until age 50, then, after just forty days in the desert of his soul, suddenly free? Can you imagine someone who, all his adult life, had never been in full control of his own mind and his own actions, then, aware the compulsion has vanished, suddenly in full control? Can you imagine the sense of loving obligation one would have for the One who had given such total freedom after such long imprisonment? I literally owed Him my life both in the removal of the addiction that had led me to the brink of suicide and in being born again to a new life, that I could only think of as heaven on earth. My constant prayer became, "Father, that I may be aware of your presence with me every moment of every day for the rest of my life." I didn't have to wait long for the answer.

The initial answer in a word was JOY! He was with me in the joy of my new freedom; and, from then on, adversity from life's challenges would never be able to take my joy. I had never known such total freedom. Though, at that time, I had been successfully self-employed in the money business for a long time, with my own office and my own secretary, a good income, debt free other than business and living expenses, able to come and go whenever I wanted, a bachelor, free in the eyes of the world; yet, I had been in prison.

Circumstances No Longer Rule

In my business the seesaw emotions experienced by most salesmen became more level and my performance and economic results immediately improved. My emotional peaks came from encounters with God and from seeing his fruit produced through me and within me, no longer from the work that earned my livelihood. In the past, my spiritual life consisted of occasions, when I would experience God's presence; but, most of the time, my focus was on the world which made me vulnerable to its entrapments. Other than for my addiction, I truly was a good person, as in the Jekyll-Hyde syndrome we previously discusssed.

Anybody can be a good person without being born again. But the emotional well being of those not reborn will depend on circumstances experienced in the world. It will depend on family relationships, work, school, social connections, etc. The measure of success or failure, of pleasure or misery, will be the yardstick of the world. There's a saying, "Don't sweat the small stuff." After rebirth, it truly all becomes small stuff in comparison to the love relationship between God and man. We no longer have to work at trying to please God as we realize His love for us is unaffected by our performance. His desire is simply that we surrender to Him and allow Him to love others through us. After my rebirth in 1990, my first experience with this was the writing of *40 Days to Freedom*.

Investing Time

I believe it important, for anyone wanting to consciously live in the presence of God, to intentionally get an early start each day. What I thought of as saturating myself in God's strength with study, meditation, and prayer started early in the morning, daily, for each day of that first forty day walk and has established this healthful habit within me ever since. This was an additional benefit to implementing that God-sent procedure.

As already shared, about a month after my healing, came the persuading to write *40 Days to Freedom*. At the time, I was rising at 5:00 A.M. each morning; and rather than change my routine to write the book, it seemed natural to get up an hour earlier. This also appealed to my sense of efficiency to waste less time in bed and spend more time in productivity. Though I can't remember my bedtime nine years ago, I suspect God compensated for my earlier rising, at least partially, at the other end of the day.

Before starting *The Man in the Desert*, my usual rising time had remained 4:00 A.M. with bedtime by 10:00 P.M. For this writing, that has been adjusted to 2:00 A.M. and 8:30 P.M. with one or two ten minute catnaps during the day. My point in disclosing all this is, if we surrender to God's will for the performing of His tasks or for seeking oneness with Him or for whatever His purpose, He will equip us; and it will seem natural and even desirable.

I share this because the modern-day excuse is "I don't have time." Well, if we are truthful, we are always able to make time for things we really desire. With God it truly is easy if we surrender control to Him. He will adapt us, lovingly, to His needs; and He will provide both the desire and the time.

So in my first writing, I enjoyed "earlier to bed, earlier to rise;" and I especially enjoyed how that earlier time was spent because it was, as now, saturated with the presence of the Spirit of God. At that time, I thought of the experience as being on fire with the Holy Spirit as I wrote every morning. Then as now, it almost seemed as if I was taking dictation; and, since I type slowly, often, I was challenged to keep up with the flow of words.

God Through Us

As I typed, God was, as validated through the many written and verbal testimonies shared through the *Freedom Letter* and our web site (www.40days2freedom.org), loving others through me. In addition, He was loving me, during the work, with an intense awareness of His presence and, after the work, by allowing me to see the fruits of His labor through me in the healed and reborn lives. Though my giving was in obedience to the direction of the One I love above all, in gratitude for all the gifts, all my life, including my life, and most especially, at that time, my rebirth, without thought of receiving, the reward of consciously experiencing His presence in the writing and in the fruits was beyond any treasure my heart could desire and has remained so.

Today, I am blessed with the knowledge that the answer to my prayer seeking that continuous, conscious awareness is "yes." Though, with the exception of producing the quarterly *Freedom Letter*, there has been a gap of about seven years between the two books, I believe the writing will continue now for as long as I am able, to which I can only respond, "Praise

God!" The seven years between books were for the further preparation needed for this work and those to follow; and, to my knowledge, the Freedom Letter will continue sharing the joy of the testimonies of blessings received through the works of this ministry. I believe all my writing in the future, as in the past and present, will be focused on freedom of the human spirit. Anyone interested in receiving the Freedom Letter can send their address to *Freedom Ministries, Inc.* via our web site (www.40days2freedom.org) which provides an e-mail link to us in addition to our mailing address. Please include your e-mail address if possible.

We enjoy the conscious awareness of the presence of God whenever we give unselfishly; in fact, that good feeling cannot be avoided. And, what we are feeling is God loving us as we love. We're not talking of token giving in the collection plate at church but meaningful, significant in our eyes, joyful giving, giving because we realize we are blessed, giving because we are touched by the need of others. This may involve money to churches or other humanitarian causes or property other than money. But, I believe, we experience what I think of as internal hugging by God when we give of ourselves and our time.

Prison Ministry

Through Kairos Prison Ministry, I participate with teams of about fifty men and women each, from mixed Christian denominations, in putting on three day retreat weekends in state and federal prisons in Central Florida. Many of these team members have participated in twenty or more of these weekends where we are simply bringing the love of Christ to the inmates. We go into the prisons on Thursday, late afternoon, and remain until Sunday evening. Some prisons, because of inmate work schedules, will only allow these retreats on holiday weekends.

The three days is the climax of a three month period of team preparation, of building a family of love to love. Over and over again, the team members give witness to the love experience of Kairos and the power of its drawing, initially, the team together into a cohesive family unit and, then, drawing the prisoners who, during their weekends, become members of the same family.

The presence of God, through agape love, is the glue that binds us all together and makes us anxious to return to team preparation and weekly meetings after a three month break after the completion of the retreat.

Each team member must agree in advance to return to the prison once a month for a minimum of one year for group meetings with the prisoners, usually on a week night, for fellowship, song, and prayer. As you can see, these team members, who come from all walks of life, poor, rich, laborers, professionals, retired people, Catholics, and Protestants, give of themselves, their time, their money, their talents, to be conduits of God's love to those on the inside who mostly have been unloved, deserted by family and society, for the crimes they've committed.

Through Kairos and other wonderful prison ministries, society is beginning to understand that more than punishment and isolation, or even training to develop work skills, is needed. Rather than being a deterrent to crime, the purely secular approach has resulted in the highest recidivism rate in history. Kairos has demonstrated the way to take the crime out of the criminal is to change his heart from one of hate and unforgiveness to a heart of love. Through Kairos and other prison ministries and prison ministers, God uses agape love to do just that. If a prisoner truly has the eyes of Jesus when he leaves prison, he won't return as a prisoner. Many have returned as prison ministers, praise God!

Now, before you're tempted to say, "I could never do that, go into prisons and give unconditional love to prisoners," I'll remind you God will equip those, who surrender to Him, to serve. I'll also remind you, according to Jesus in the *Bible* and as stated elsewhere in this work, God expects us to love the unlovables, the prisoners, the homeless, the destitute, the sick, the elderly, and all the disadvantaged in this world. I often wonder if the very reason for the existence of so many in need is that they be loved by the many who have such abundance. The great mystery is the givers are the ones who benefit the most, not just in the world to come, but also in the here and now. Just ask any volunteer who works with any of the unlovables; and you'll receive the same answer.

God's Presence

Due to the direct effect of the Kairos, agape love procedure, over a twenty year period in the state prisons of Florida, a new law was recently signed, enhancing cooperation between prison administrations and volunteer organizations, offering the spiritual approach to rehabilitation. In a way, I saw this as the first reversal of the ridiculous enforcement of separation of God and government, referred to as separation of church and state, which law, to my understanding, was originally devised to protect churches and religion from intrusion by government, not the reverse.

I'm not saying religion is necessary to Godliness. I am saying freedom of religious expression enhances Godliness and enhances our society in all its facets. To say that religious expression is improper in schools, in the workplace, in prisons, and in government is ridiculous as long as it is not being imposed on others. In other words no one should feel pressured to pray or join a religion; and, frankly, the abuse of some religions and denominations have helped create our secular society.

I am saying that prayer and other religious expression can help us to be more aware of God's presence in our lives. The more aware we are of His presence, the more connected to Him we remain and the less vulnerable to the harmful temptations of the world, which lead to our disconnecting from God and gravitating toward greed, pride, lust, and other ways contrary to love. In recent times such gravitating has led to hate crimes resulting in substantial loss of innocent lives.

When we remain aware of God's presence in our lives, we are instilled with a sense of peace and contentment regardless of our circumstances. Challenges will always be there for us; but, instead of dreading them, we can recognize them for what they are, opportunities for growth in knowledge and awareness of God. This scenario is conducive to brotherhood and is possible for the entire world. The only uniting force which can lead to such brotherhood of humankind is God who is Love. He alone is our common link to each other. Our sonship and daughtership in Him truly makes us all brothers and sisters, regardless of race, religion, or other worldly differences, created to be brothers and sisters in love with Him and each other.

This is truly the only path to the world peace which has proved so illusive to all governments in the past. This is the only way, the way Jesus taught us, the wars and crimes of cruelty will stop. We truly can all live together on this planet, still worshipping God in our own unique ways, with or without organized religion, still cherishing our traditions and ethnic backgrounds, but, all the time in love and peace. It's our choice; we can do it; but we can't do it without God; and He won't force us to do it. Jesus will not come on a cloud and single-handedly wipe out all the sin in the world. We humans created sin and God expects us to eliminate it <u>with His help</u>. Human weakness subject to temptation, through centuries of spiritual evolving away from God, makes us incapable of living in peace without Him. The way of love, the path back to God, will yield all our hearts' desires for ourselves and our children.

Children of God

If we shower our children with materialism and secular education and don't educate them about their spiritual lives and common heritage in God, we do them a great injustice which, I believe, for each parent, one day will return to haunt us. This is true in my own life, though religion was a part of our children's upbringing, I can see now that religious practices alone are not enough to instill a knowledge of the divine. Children need to be informed, at an early age, about their inner voice, their *Internal Bible*, the wonderful knowledge of their Creator Father, given by Him to serve them all their lives and to bring them back home to Him; and, most of all, they need to be loved, really loved, unselfishly loved.

As adults, we need to see ourselves as children, children of the Most High, and, thus, blessed children, subject to His nurturing, if we will but accept it, all our lives. As when we are children of our biological parents on earth, and as we commune

135

with them every day in our youth, we also need to commune, every day, with our Heavenly Father, all our lives. Agape love, prayer, study, and fellowship are the primary ways God has given us to tune in to His presence with us every day. Tune in to His presence because He is always with us; but we aren't always aware of the presence of His great Spirit which is truly omnipresent, which truly envelopes us, all the time, without which we could not draw our next breath or cause our heart to beat its next beat.

God's Orchestration

The Spirit, the active energy of God's soul, permeates the universe and orchestrates its functioning in perfect harmony. Did you know, with our earth ninety-six million miles from our sun, that, if we were just one hundred twenty-five miles closer, we could not exist? Did you know that, if we were just one hundred twenty-five miles further away, likewise, again, we could not exist?

Is there, somewhere out there, another speck in this gigantic sea of space that has just the right circumstance to support life in any form that resembles what we enjoy here? I have been a Star Trek fan for many years and, by choice, was a science and math major in college. But, did you know that the margin for error, as calculated by a top US mathematician, in the evolution of the universe to the point where life exists, as it does today, on this tiny planet is so small that the denominator of the fraction, with a numerator of one, is the largest number ever calculated by man and has been presented as scientific evidence that the belief that no managing, creating intelligence, or God exists requires more faith than believing there is such a being? The closer I grow to the Father, the more I learn about Him, the more in awe of Him I am.

Silent Presence

Other than moments of spiritual awakening or transformation, my closest times with the Father are during contemplative prayer. In 1994, a monk came from Snowmass, Colorado, to my church in Central Florida, to conduct a workshop. I knew this to be a very quiet meditative prayer form and anticipated the same in the demeanor of our teacher. I was surprised by one of the most dynamic speakers I've experienced. Yet, with his expressed enthusiasm there was this peace, this calm, this quiet confidence that made me want to be like him. Through his guidance, I discovered what was to become my primary prayer form and an important key to my desire to consciously live in God's presence.

Meditation, centering prayer, and contemplative prayer are the main forms of this method of coming into quiet communion with God. There are minor differences in the technical aspects of focus and use of a prayer word or mantra; but I refer to the method I practice as contemplative prayer. What I most remember about Father Meninger's teaching is the benevolence of God, that we don't have to be perfect in our focus or concentration as God is simply pleased that we give Him this time. Interruptions are not cause for anxiety as we can simply leave the prayer to attend to the distraction, if necessary, and calmly return. In this prayer we don't worry about who or what God is; we simply acknowledge He is and our love for Him. A prayer word may be used to help one eliminate the world from the thoughts and mind and come to an awareness of His presence. As the focus of the mind is on loving God, I have used a prayer word of "Jesus," considering a father's joy in hearing the name of his son, as an expression of love. I have also used "Father" as a prayer word; though my prayer word has been displaced by a quiet groan of longing, almost a chant, as I think of it.

Though this prayer is one of great solitude and going within, as Jesus instructed, it is often done on a group basis. It would seem that fellowship before and after the prayer and the discipline of group support are the primary motivations for this coming together. I, personally, rarely join groups for this purpose as in 1995 I saw this prayer form so important in my quest of consciousness of God, that I used the procedure in *40 Days to Freedom* to establish the daily habit.

I will do my best in trying to describe my experience when in this prayer. Most often, I am either in the sauna at my health club or sitting on the couch in my office which, currently, is also my home. With eyes closed, I attempt to go within; though I am usually unable to block thought patterns; but this no longer brings frustration as I have learned that the mind and the soul are distinct entities and my soul can be focused on God while my mind involuntarily is elsewhere. Sometimes, while in this prayer, God will use these mind wanderings to communicate important messages to me which was my experience with the three messages that came with the full-time calling to ministry. Soon after starting, the quiet groaning will begin without conscious effort on my part. I believe this to be the action of my soul; and, again, it has replaced my use of a prayer word.

No matter the extent of wandering thoughts, at about eight minutes into the prayer, I become suddenly aware of God's presence; and my mind is drawn to the focus of my soul which is on loving and anticipating God. Soon after, a vision of clouds appears. They are always in motion, going out, coming in, or rolling. As the prayer proceeds I am aware that God is loving me and a beautiful violet color appears in the vision. Often, there is a small intense light in the middle of a rolling cloud. The vision has come to represent to me a dancing or mingling of my spirit with God's. The experience, though often intense, always leaves me with a great peace and knowledge of God's presence with me and a sense of His great love for me to the extent I think of this process as my romance with Him. It is more fulfilling than any experience I have ever had with another human being. The total time involved in this romantic, prayer interlude, for me, is generally less than twenty minutes.

In contemplative prayer, as in other encounters with God, an attitude of love, trust, and surrender is necessary. He has proven His benevolence to me by answering my desire for conscious awareness of His presence in spite of my mind wandering in the process. Here again, God is saying, "It is not human perfection I seek but heart-felt desire."

Emotions

So often today, religion relies on group song to create an emotional group response. This can be used or abused. If the only way a religious leader can reach his audience with his message is by creating a fervor through song, then the message is not standing on its own and may not be the truth. The truth needs no prepping or advance stimulation in order to be recognized or received. If the truth is indeed being preached or taught, the *Internal Bible* of the recipient is enough to recognize it. I am not saying songs or hymns are wrong; or that they shouldn't be used in worship as I personally enjoy such participation. But if music is our main draw to a service, it's possible for a manipulation of emotion to be used to sell other than truth. Such services should not be used as a replacement for quiet prayer where God is being sought in solitude within, as Jesus taught.

Man manipulates; God orchestrates. Man continuously tries to remake God in his image. God offers man His essence if man will but seek, of his own free will, to become more like God. "Seek and you will find," we were told by the greatest man who ever lived. If we do not seek, we will not find. The bestowal of divinity is not automatic. The butterfly must seek to break the shell of its cocoon to realize the transformation offered it. Likewise, man must seek to break his earthly mold, must seek his transformation, his rebirth into the new creature he was intended to be from his creation. For man, rebirth is just the beginning of a wonderful process that culminates, in God's time, in his becoming the divine angel. But man may choose to remain mortal man; and most will.

Soul Progression on Earth

Our method of seeking is simple; we need no intercessors. We are always in the Father's presence; and, though we can't see Him with our physical eyes, we can see Him with the eyes of our soul and, even better after our rebirth, when they become the eyes of Jesus. And we can be aware of His presence. This is beneficial, not only for our heavenly future after leaving our physical bodies, but for the immediate present. Though probation and growth continue after body death, Jesus in Padgett tells us conversion is more difficult after passing to the spirit world. Since we are generally better off there, unimcumbered by physical limitations, we have more of a tendency to settle for what we have and where we are.

This may seem good to be content. It may seem a contradiction to aspire to more than we have and to become more than we are. Ambition is not necessarily a bad thing if it is motivated by love; and, in the sense presented here and in Padgett, it is motivated by the highest love and the highest selflessness; for in seeking to become the Divine Angel we are seeking to surrender our will for God's, our mind for God's, our love for God's. We are seeking to cast off all that separates us from our Creator Father so we may more perfectly serve Him for eternity.

If, all of our earthly lives, we remain focused on things, beings, and challenges of this world and do not develop a God mind-set and soul-set, we are less likely to do so in the spirit world. Jesus relates in Padgett that our time on earth is our most important development time in this regard. If we do not enter the cocoon of focusing on God while here, we are less likely to do so after leaving; and, he, in fact, relates that the vast majority of men and women will settle for the happiness of the spirit world and not seek the eternal bliss of the Celestial Heavens. I would put forth that, by so settling, we are exercising a form of greed and selfishness, that we are rebelling against the will of God by becoming less than we can be.

Man's quality of ambition is an indicator of this. As with other gifts, we often misuse it and apply it for self fulfillment rather than fulfillment of divine purpose. Truly, the opposite of ambition, sloth or laziness, regarded as one of the seven deadly sins, is very different from contentment. We can strive, by living in God's presence, to be all we can be, as His servants, allowing Him to live and work though us, and, at the same time, be content with that role. Ambition, simplicity, and contentment can all exist together and more, thrive together, in a soul reborn in the Divine Love of the Father.

Godliness and Normality

There is a saying, "misery loves company," which may seem correct. Certainly, man has painted the myth of the fallen angel who is seeking to fill his habitat with as many souls as possible to accompany him though his eternity of hell. But, I believe, the opposite is more true. I believe joy loves company! I believe this is evidenced in God wanting us with Him in His domain, the Holy of Holies, the Celestial Heavens, to share His joy for eternity. I believe this is evidenced on earth by those who truly live consciously in His presence, being the most joyful, contented, peaceful people; yet they also have this ambition to serve God in many ways, all reflecting His love.

Age is no barrier here. This is a matter of focus. We can be active, normal children, adolescents, young adults, middle-aged, senior, or elderly. No matter the stage of our life, it will be better, more enjoyable, more fruitful, for us and for all the people we touch with our life. We can be blessings at any age instead of being consumers. What an indictment that term is on humanity. Yet we have accepted, seemingly without insult, being referred to as consumers.

When I said we can be Godly and be normal at the same time, I wasn't referring to normal in the eyes of our present world; but, if we want the world to be a safer, better place for our children, then Godly must become normal; or we will end our earthly lives in our own destruction.

Agape

Rather than being consumers we need to become givers. This doesn't mean we all stop consuming and our economy grinds to a halt. No, it means we just start giving a little more than we take. Tithing ten percent of our income out of Biblical obligation doesn't make us givers. In fact, we can become Scrooges with such giving. But, if we assess our total lives, including our family, work, religion, and community, and give fifty-one percent of our total abundance which is all from God, including time, effort, enthusiasm, money, and, most of all, love, while we consume forty-nine percent, then we are more givers than consumers. Of course, we don't have to stop at fifty-one percent as our role model gave one hundred percent. We needn't worry that we'll give ourselves out of existence as Jesus and others in the *Bible* tell us we can't outgive God.

141

Even with secular jobs, we can give one hundred percent through an attitude of love and service to all those we touch instead of an attitude of "I need a pay raise" or "Is it time to go home yet?" If we are givers in the workplace, the pay raises will take care of themselves and the time will fly.

Here again, our giving must be properly motivated, must be agape, joyful giving, leaving the results for others and ourselves in God's capable hands. Here again, we are returning to surrender and trust, as if we were little children, depending totally on our Parent for our provision of everything including life itself. We are His children and we do depend on Him whether we consciously admit it or not.

Opportunity in Adversity

My experience in growing in the conscious awareness of God's loving presence has been the greatest blessing of my life. He has proven His constant love and concern for me over and over again, through all the years, by guiding me through every challenge, even when I wasn't aware of His guidance. Probably, at about age thirty two, was my first real awareness of how supporting and present He is, when I marveled at how my family and I had not only survived the death of my military career four years earlier, but we were, in truth, better for it. Only God is the orchestrator of changing adversity to blessing.

Now, as I continue to grow in the new life He gave me nine years ago, there is no longer adversity, only challenge to continue in that growth toward greater oneness with Him. The rewards are both overwhelming and lasting as they will remain with me for eternity, never rusting, never wearing out, never spending out. In the final analysis, the rewards all boil down to simple expression of His love, the greatest of which is sharing His very essence with me. What an awesome God!

The gifts come with no strings attached, no consideration for the results of my dedication and efforts, as that depends on their acceptance by humanity, which is free to either accept or reject. But my rewards are not based on humanity's acceptance of His message through me, any more than was Jesus' reward two thousand years ago. If we simply surrender, trust, obey, seek, and love, this is all that is required. This is why we are here to find our way back home to the place of our creation. Like the salmon we can make this trip, which seems impossible to many, but becomes easy when we leave the swimming, the traversing, to Him by following the teaching of the one He sent as His son.

We can ignore His presence if we wish; but that doesn't make Him any less present; or us any less dependent on Him. By immersing ourselves in His presence, we both insulate ourselves from the hazards of the world and open ourselves to a joy and peace and freedom which will never cease to amaze us. Praise God!

VII. HEAVEN AND HELL

Harmony

Being reborn in the Divine Love Essence of God had been available to Adam and Eve, or whom they represent, until their fall or disobedience. Jesus announced that the gates to the Celestial Heavens were now reopened and would remain open until the day of judgment or consummation. The *Bible* reference to the "separation of the sheep from the goats" is clarified in the Padgett Messages as the end of the bestowal of the potential for spiritual rebirth. That day is only known to the Father and may not yet be fixed by Him.

Does this mean, since this is effectively the closing of the gates of heaven, that God is limiting His love for us to a chosen number as some would say the *Bible* indicates? I don't believe so. If we humans knew that the gates would remain open forever, we could be tempted to procrastinate seeking rebirth forever. God is not in the temptation business. Though He allows it, He does not create it. I once read that the phrase, "Lead us not into temptation," in the Lord's Prayer was a misinterpretation due to language differences. I must admit I had always been uncomfortable with this part of the prayer and now realize the discomfort originated in my *Internal Bible*. Somehow I knew God would not lead us into temptation but would allow us to be tempted that our free will might be exercised. "Leave us not in temptation" was presented as the proper translation which is the way I now say and mean the prayer.

In addition, harmony for the universe is one of God's laws which has been broken by man, through sin and error; and, therefore, all sin and error will be eliminated. This is a part of God's plan for the universe and for man. The hells of the spirit world are real, real places and real circumstances of torment and darkness, which may be experienced for a long time according to our decisions and lives on earth; but, because of God's laws, which are unchangeable, the spirit spheres of hell are temporary.

145

Therefore, all souls will eventually occupy the heaven of the spirit world or the Celestial Heavens of God.

This does not mean we can live our lives lustfully, pridefully, and greedily without paying the consequences. Indeed, another of God's laws as referenced by Jesus is we will reap what we sow. This too is unchangeable; and it is not canceled by a deathbed profession of faith. We enter the spirit world in the soul condition in which we leave earth. Jesus confirms in Padgett that even those who are reborn, who subsequently backslide, will experience hell before heaven. He also relates that any place that is not heaven is hell which would include what Catholics think of as purgatory, a concept based on truth since probation and progression of soul condition do not end with physical death. We therefore can conclude that, as soon as we backslide and are thus out of harmony with God's laws, we are indeed in hell, hopefully without fire and brimstone, which is another of man's myths.

Hell on Earth?

Can we be on earth and in hell at the same time? I think the reality of the truth will hit most readers as they read the question. We know that heaven involves a perpetual sense of joy and peace as basic attributes which would indicate many if not most inhabitants of this physical world are experiencing other than heaven. This further fits, I believe, as Jesus indicated in the *Bible*, his kingdom is not this earth. In Padgett he confirms it is the Celestial Heavens of God. Most people on earth therefore are, at the same time, in hell with the particular level or sphere determined by the degree of one's torment or darkness. The good news of Jesus in Padgett is that hell is not eternal for any soul.

I also believe, when our physical bodies die, our heaven or hell experience is intensified as we enter the spirit world shed of the limitations of our earthly bodies. Jesus in Padgett refers to total recall of our life on earth experience as part of our freeing process in leaving the physical world. We can imagine this may add to either our joy or our suffering.

Heaven, One or Two or Three?

Can we be on earth and in heaven at the same time? Or more, can we be on earth and in the Celestial Heavens at the same time? These are perhaps more challenging questions for the reader; but, before we answer, let's look at the different heavens before us.

In Padgett, Jesus defines the highest heaven of the spirit world in terms of the human understanding of Paradise involving joy and peace beyond anything we can imagine. Here we are restored to the created soul condition of our original parents of humanity on earth with our God-given natural love in perfect harmony with His laws. We attain this by progressing in growth and improvement in our soul condition which may start on earth but certainly will start after entry to the spirit world though not necessarily immediately.

As when we are in the flesh, we can be influenced by good or evil spirits; and, in this regard, like attracts like. So we may continue to try to fulfill our human lusts after departing our physical bodies; but, of course, we will be hampered in doing so which will add to our torment and may cause us to be one of those attempting to influence those in the flesh in evil ways to attempt to live out our desires through their bodies.

In spite of all this, the spirits from higher spheres will attempt to lead us to repent and reform. As the evil spirits, eventually, see the light, so to speak, they are led out of their darkness and begin to progress, some faster than others, depending on their degree of disharmony. The progression continues until the spirit reaches the highest sphere of the spirit world where, unless the spirit has been reborn, soul development stops, as the natural love of the individual has been perfected, as with our original human parents before their fall into disobedience. Here, the person, the soul clad in spirit body, continues a wonderful existence but does not have knowledge of personal immortality which only comes through rebirth and ascent to the Celestial Heavens. Until the Day of Judgment this spirit has the same opportunity to seek the Divine Love as all others in the spirit world and on earth.

You might at this point ask why would not everyone attaining this degree of perfection seek rebirth through the Holy Spirit? In the spirit world, as on earth, people have their own opinions and views and are not easily persuaded to change especially if they are relatively happy and content where they are. The only path to the Celestial Heavens is through seeking the Divine Love of God, oneness with God, with true soul longing or hunger for God.

It would seem to this writer, after daily study of *The Celestial Testament of Jesus*, for well over a year that, where humans are concerned, God will employ every effort to not invade His great gift of free will. Therefore, as on earth, if we settle for where we are and what we have, if we do not seek, we will not find. It also seems to me an element of risk is involved, at least superficially, where the soul may be afraid of losing what has already been attained as on earth. I have observed even some incarcerated, over many years of prison ministry, resisting change, though they're miserable, as if they fear giving up something worthwhile to progress toward God.

God will never ask us to sacrifice anything that is truly worthwhile. Even in the story of Job, his freedom was maintained; his life was maintained; his growth in soul development continued during his suffering. By persisting through his suffering, all that was sacrificed was more than recovered. Of course, Jesus is the greatest example. He literally sacrificed everything in the eyes of the world; but it was all relatively unimportant in comparison to the truth to which he held steadfastly. By sacrificing the most and through obedience unto death, he received the greatest reward and left physical proof behind that we might be inspired to follow. Though Christians and others stand in awe at what he gave that we might be free, what he gave was relatively unimportant in comparison to what he achieved and received. We can absolutely trust God that this will always be so if we remain firm with our focus and desire fixed on Him.

Because of God's respect for our freedom, it's as if we must convince Him of our total surrender to Him. I believe this may be why so many people seem to reach their turning point or conversion or even rebirth through desperate situations as was true with this writer. When we get desperate, we get honest. We become desperate for God and He responds. This is the path to rebirth; but we must be willing to sacrifice what is not worthwhile for what is. We must be willing to put absolute trust in the Father and absolute faith that He wants only what is best for us. This is true even when he is using us for His purpose with others as if we are His angels, which we can be, whether in the flesh, in the spirit world, or in the Celestial Heavens. We cannot help but benefit from doing His work. Ask any prison minister, who benefits more from his or her work, the prisoners or them? I promise a uniform answer of no doubt but they, the ministers of God's love to the unloved, receive the greater blessing.

We keep repeating ourselves, "God is love." Praise God! Though He will not violate our free will, He will allow us to surrender it; and, for those who surrender it to Him, He, through His Holy Spirit and Jesus the Christ, has prepared a place called, by Jesus in Padgett, the Celestial Heavens or, in the *Bible*, many rooms in his Father's house. This is the domain of the divine only. For all who seek the Lord their God, His Divine Love, oneness with Him, true desire to surrender free will for God's will, with all their hearts and all their souls and all their minds and all their strength, this is their final home, a home where there is no end to progress in peace, in joy, in love, in knowledge of God, in soul development closer to Him. In the Celestial Heavens, with God there is always more.

At the decision of the Father; and I believe it unique with each individual, when He decides, we are ready we make this quantum leap this final conversion from mortal human to Divine Angel. Then, His will becomes our will; His mind our mind; His love our love. This final leap is beyond freedom; though without freedom it cannot be sought. It is beyond definition except, that upon passing through this portal, we know we are immortal; and we know our destiny is to live and love and serve forever, ever growing closer to the Source of all that is good.

This is not to say those in the spirit world heaven will not live forever; but, according to Jesus in Padgett, immortality includes knowledge of immortality which we cannot have outside of the Celestial Heavens. Jesus also relates that the Father betrays nothing if man, who remains man only, should someday cease to exist as he was never guaranteed immortality to begin with. Man's speculation or stating that all men are immortal does not make it so.

Knowledge of the Truth

God alone is the origin of all truth even as testified by Jesus according to the *Bible*. Further, according to Jesus in Padgett, truth is not dependent on the knowledge of man to be truth. Jesus further testified, according to the *Bible* and Padgett, that not all truth had been disclosed to even him by the Father.

In Padgett, he continues to grow closer to the Father as his highest Divine Angel. And, perhaps the best news, of all the "good news" in the *Bible*, is we can be like him; though, I suspect it unlikely that any will achieve his heights as Jesus is the Master of the Celestial Heavens. If you should be led to study the Padgett Messages (www.divine.org), you will discover Jesus to be a most gracious, humble though authoritative, loving master unlike the Jesus purportedly communicating through some others in these times.

Through Padgett, Jesus discloses the truth about the last days, Christian Science, reincarnation, the church, God, heaven and hell, the after-life, the Apostles, love, and so much more. The information is all public domain. Here, as with my other sources for this work, I am presenting only what is directed by the Father's Spirit and from memory, in my own words, rather than direct quotes. I therefore encourage the reader to study Padgett and the other sources in the Acknowledgments to draw his or her own enlightenment. Keep in mind, as you study, the times when these other works were created and the changes in humankind and the world since their creation. For example, I have seen substantial evolution in the Catholic Church in my lifetime. The truth never changes; but its application may change as we change and grow closer to its Source.

We must beware the false messiahs. But we must also beware being close-minded as some religious leaders and teachers. Such teaching is not motivated by God but by selfish purpose of man to control man. WE CAN TRUST GOD. Through the *Internal Bible* He has given every one of us, we have the ability to discern the truth without intermediaries if we simply seek the Father's guidance.

Though I consider the method of information conveyance through Padgett more reliable than other methods, including those of the writers of the *Bible*, it is not the method but the messages themselves that have convinced me of their truth. Some may say a year's study of the fifty-two messages of length of about one of the Gospels of the New Testament is not enough to make such bold proclamations. I can only answer that I believe God has been preparing me over my lifetime starting with Christine Doctrine at age five or six, study of the *Bible* more focused on New Testament than Old and more focused on the Four Gospels, the words of Jesus. I would also include a wealth of Christian Literature, most notably the works of Thomas Merton, and the study of what I regard as the one perfect Gospel of Jesus, the Shroud of Turin.

But more important than the literature has been the people and the life experience itself. I humbly admit to a special qualification as a lost soul who tasted the depths of hell to the very brink of self-destruction. But for the grace of my loving Father, I would not now be alive to write this; but, without that experience, as without the crucifixion of Jesus, this message could not be; for in His wisdom God allowed the challenges and orchestrated my growth out of them, gave me rebirth in His Divine love and the eyes of Jesus that I may clearly see and discern the truth through the gift of my *Internal Bible*. He saved me from self-destruction. He freed me from my bondage of forty years in the desert. He directed me to write *40 Days to Freedom*. He directed me to write *The Man in the Desert*.

Every day, He showers me with His love in an intimacy I have attempted to describe but can do no justice. A year's study of the Celestial Testament and the wealth of accompanying and corroborating information is not enough and I plan to spend the rest of my eternal life in studying Padgett and all information that will further reveal the knowledge and truth of God. You see, I have this hunger, this great hunger for Him, that will never be satisfied, but always eager, and the quest always fulfilling, according to His grace and His plan for me. And so may it be for each of us.

Living in God, and allowing Him to live in and through us, is a life filled with adventure and great discovery every day. When I was self-employed in the financial business, I planned everything out in detail in advance. When I did not get the desired results, there was frustration. When I did, there was elation but short lived; for there was always pressure from within and from without to achieve more; and reaching the goal was never quite as fulfilling as it was supposed to be. Now, though in the eyes of the world I work alone for the most part, I no longer have the pressure of being self-employed and self-dependent or independent. I simply surrender and wait for direction from my Boss who happens to also be my Lover and my Father. What more privileged situation can one have?

I need do almost no planning except for what is required of an author in the world; and I probably could do less of that if my trust was more perfect. This morning was an example as I started working shortly after 3:00 A.M. I had a wonderful, inspired writing session; and, before I knew it, the time was 4:15 A.M., which meant time to stretch, hop on my bicycle to the health club, and lap swim. I suddenly realized that this was my plan, a good plan, but not necessarily the best plan, so I surrendered to my inner voice and went back to the computer, where I experienced a more wonderful, more inspired second writing session until 6:45 A.M., when I stopped to fix breakfast. Usually, after breakfast I do a few housekeeping chores, necessary since I live in my office, and then start into ministry business, correspondence, and so on; but, you guessed it, not this morning. By 7:30 A.M. back on the computer sharing this with you now.

What I'm saying is, though the world still sees me as self-employed, I live in an entirely different world than before; and my peace and elation and sense of discovery, as this morning, is becoming my norm. No planning, no goals or, I should say, worldly goals, no stress, just relaxed obedience, leaving the results of my efforts entirely to my Boss. Do you think there is anyone on earth with whom I would trade places?

Don't misunderstand, this level of being, of living, of attitude is not reserved only for Christian authors but for anyone in any vocation or avocation where service to God or man or both is possible. To me, it is heaven on earth which brings us back to the topic of this chapter and the close of this writing session as I am pleasurably tired. Oh, for the health buffs, Father will still allow my workout today. He just tweaked the schedule a little.

Earlier in this chapter, we posed two questions: can we be on earth and in heaven at the same time; and, can we be on earth and in the Celestial Heavens at the same time? From what followed and from elsewhere in this work, the reader can see I believe that I am both in the physical world and in heaven as a state of being. I do not claim to yet reside in the Celestial Heavens though I have had such powerful encounters with the Holy Spirit, with the inflowing of God's Divine Love so overwhelming, that, especially at one time, I believed the final transformation to Divine Angel had occurred.

I do have confidence that, since I am growing in the Divine Love, I will one day enter the Celestial Heavens of God; and look forward to a growing oneness with Him for all eternity. In Padgett, Jesus indicates the possibility, though a rarity, of the transformation to Divine Angel while in the flesh. He, as we earlier stated, was the first. I believe, possibly, his apostles and relatively few others have since. From Padgett we know many others have progressed to the Celestial Heavens, after leaving the flesh, as well as many who walked the earth before Jesus. St. Paul refers to cities within the spheres of the Celestial Heavens; but I am still left with the feeling, in comparison to all the souls ever incarnated, relatively few had entered at least at the time of the Padgett Messages.

Evidence has been presented, by Jesus and by other Divine Angels, of God's benevolence in that specific knowledge or procedure is less important than the desire of the soul for oneness with the Father and the expressed hunger of the soul to receive His Divine Love. In this regard, St. John indicated in Padgett that a moment of sincere soul longing is worth more than hours of words from the intellect. Also presented is testimony of those who experienced darkness in the Spirit World, related to their lives on earth, who now reside in the heavens of the divine.

Jesus teaches that such darkness can be experienced even by those who are unknowingly doing wrong. He shows that separation from God's laws creates disharmony and creates the hell experience; and ignorance is not a factor, except that those, who unintentionally err, will progress more rapidly out of the darkness into the light than those who have willfully disobeyed. Further, the only path into the light is through repentance and conversion back into God's harmony. This path is available to everyone and the angels from the spirit heavens and from the Celestial Heavens are there to help. Also, it is worth restating, the only path to oneness with the Father is through Jesus' teaching of the New Birth which is in accord with the *Bible*.

The concept that in heaven we all have nothing to do all day but sing "glory" is wrong. The angels of the heavens as on earth have the purpose of helping others and progressing in their own soul development; and they take great joy, as Jesus indicates in the *Bible*, in the saving of lost souls. Of course, a soul is never totally or permanently lost; and, from the standpoint of all eventually residing in either the highest heaven of the spirit world or the Celestial Heavens, all will be saved. Thus we can assume that one who claims to be an agnostic, yet lives in love, will know heaven before one who claims to be a Christian yet lives in hate or arrogance or judgmentalism or unforgiveness.

But, without praying to receive the Divine Love, one cannot receive it as it will not be forced. However, Jesus in Padgett states that this earnest prayer from the soul will never be refused by the Father. This is certainly the greatest news I have ever received! No matter where we are, no matter what we've done, no matter what we've believed, if we pray for and desire the Divine Love of the Father with all our hearts and with all our souls and with all our minds and with all our strength, IT WILL BE GIVEN; and we are "born again," destined to experience the final transformation of man to the Divine Angel and become residents of God's Celestial Heavens in oneness with Him! What an awesome God!

Jesus' way is the way of love, both the natural love of man received by each soul at its creation and the Divine Love of the Father received through His Holy Spirit. The perfection of the natural love can progress without receiving the Divine Love Essence of God; however, if one is born again and receives the Divine Love, the natural love will also come to eventual perfection. Again, no one is immediately transformed upon body death; we enter as we leave. As on earth, effort and influence and instruction are all needed, with the assistance of God and His team, where Jesus is the chief worker and the chief worshipper.

The Power of Prayer

I feel inspired at this point to make a special note about the importance of prayer. I believe all the great religions on earth stress this; and I believe some practice it better than Christianity. I was both impressed and motivated, all through my study of the Padgett Messages, by Jesus and the other spirits in communication with Padgett encouraging him to pray more. Communication with the Father, as I have elsewhere indicated, is of paramount importance to everyone who desires a harmonious, happy life and especially for those who seek the closest possible unity with God. Our prayer need not be perfect; but we must devote our precious commodity of time to Him. I believe this to be key.

One's entire life can be a prayer, as demonstrated by Jesus; and my opinion of a modern day example would be the recently deceased Mother Teresa. They were both living examples of a constant focus on the Father leading to acts of love for humanity and heroic though simple lives. I believe, when we are communing with God, we are insulated from evil; and, when we are not, we are vulnerable. Also, a simple life, less cluttered with the objects of affluence, allows us to more easily focus on God and His true treasures bestowed on us every day.

I believe the emphasis on prayer in the Padgett Messages will help to validate them for the discerning or critical eye. It just makes no sense that the purported enemy of God would encourage anyone to pray more to God. As Jesus asked according to Scripture, "Does Beelzebub cast out Beelzebub?" And while on this subject, we've spent significant time here talking about heaven and angels and little about the master of evil, Satan, and his demons. Let's start with evil since many would give God credit for the creation of evil which He doesn't deserve.

The Evolution of Sin

God created man to also be a creator, of course not on the same scale as the Almighty. Man is the creator of evil; but not, as some would have us believe, only in his mind. No, evil is real and is the real creation of man as is Satan. While there are evil spirits, as we have discusssed, there is no fallen angel named Lucifer who is the master of all the evil spirits while, I believe, there may exist a hierarchy or organizing intellects among those in the spirit spheres of darkness; but no Satan and no demons as separate creations of Satan or anyone else. Further, man created the first sin, which I see as a combination of pride and greed, when he committed the first act of disobedience as told in the story of Adam and Eve in the garden.

As with the other stories of the Old Testament, the exact characters and the exact circumstances are unimportant; but the story relates a powerful message for humankind. Adam and Eve were experiencing heaven on earth. Not the Celestial Heavens; but they had that potential if they pursued oneness with the Father. Before they did, they sinned and fell from grace; thereby losing their potential for rebirth in the Divine Love of God. This original sin they passed on for many generations not from the standpoint of heredity or genes but from the standpoint of an evolution of humanity growing in separation from God as it focussed more and more on on the things of this world.

Between Adam and Jesus were many emissaries from God, referred to mostly as prophets, who realized and acted on the divine purpose given each by God at the creation of their souls. These were men and women referred to in the *Bible* and the sacred texts of the other great religions. Finally, God sent a very special man, who is rightly called His first son in the *Bible*, though not His "only begotten son," which, we have presented, was the invention of man in the early centuries of Christianity. The Messiah, the Christ, and the Word (love) made flesh are all appropriate tiles. That he was special is best proved by his impact on the world and his following which has survived the errors and manipulations of man through the ages. Secondarily, it is proved by the unique photographic gospel he left, by the grace of his Father, as confirmation that love is the way and the truth and the life unto death. Though not God, Jesus was love incarnate, truth incarnate, divinity incarnate.

The Second Coming

So Jesus, the man, became the first divine son of the Father and opened the door for us to follow. He started the reversal of the spiritual evolution of man away from the Father; but he only started, as relatively few have been saved, from the standpoint of genuinely being born again in the Divine Love. Now, many expect Jesus to physically return to earth and single-handedly eradicate all sin and establish his kingdom on earth. This too is myth as it would represent the interference of God in the free will of man which He will not do! He does not violate His own laws!

Jesus has come again, in spirit, to James Padgett and has transmitted the information necessary for man to eradicate sin on earth which must happen for God's harmony to be reestablished. God will work through man and is providing the help of Jesus and the heavenly hosts in this effort; but the work must be done through man. Thus, peace on earth will be realized; but it is up to humankind when.

157

Heaven on earth will be a reality eventually for all in the flesh. Heaven in the spirit world is now a reality though the spheres of hell still exist and are fed by souls from earth. And the Celestial Heavens of God were established with Jesus as the first inhabitant and those following, only through the grace of the Father, in the sharing of His Divine Essence with mortal man. This too is Biblical as Paul referenced the existence of three heavens.

The Gates Closed

At the Father's decision, the gates to the Celestial Heavens will close as we have discusssed. This is thought of, in Christianity, as the "Day of Judgment," the day of "separation of the sheep from the goats." Those, who have not sought and received the Divine Love, by that day, as with Adam and Eve, will fall from that grace but will still be blessed to eventually reside in the spirit world heaven, as the spheres of hell will be abolished, and the complete harmony of God's universe restored, not through magic, but through the gentle persuasion of God and Jesus and the angels.

So this is the meaning of being a lost soul, though not as bad as the false teachers would have us believe, still less than we were created for. Though I write this book out of obedience to my Father and need no fulfillment other than that obedience, it is my earnest prayer that this, and other works like it, will motivate people to truly become all they can be, sons and daughters in the Divine Love Essence of our Father and residents of the Celestial Heavens established for the purpose of an eternity of joy and peace and growing closer to the One who is love.

VIII. THE THIRD MAN

Soul

As stated in the preface, this is the story of three men. The first is the author. The second, in the eyes of the author, is the greatest man who ever walked this earth, Jesus the Christ. And, in case you haven't already guessed, the third man or woman is you, the reader. So who are you? Are you young or old, man or woman, married or single, professional or laborer, rich or poor? None of this really matters because you are a child of God.

Your soul was knit by Him in heaven before you were incarnated just like mine; and, just like me, you were made to live for eternity and be not only the son or daughter of God but His friend. Gender, occupation, material wealth, etc., none of these matter, when we face eternity, because the earthly things are but for a moment, a single breath in an eternity where time and space are no constraints to the billions of occupants of the spirit world.

Angels

Just imagine, every person who has ever walked this earth, every soul ever incarnated, is still alive in the spirit world or on earth. Those in God's light are angels; and many angels are working to help humans; and many are in the earth sphere with us. Some people believe that our loved ones, who precede us to the spirit world, remain with us as guardians or help us in other ways.

In 1996, at age 69, my brother died. At the time, I was scheduled to ride my bicycle from Orlando to Miami in a fund-raiser for Aids Charities in Florida. I was to ride just days after his death but, grieving over his loss more than I had anticipated I would, considered withdrawing from the ride and, then, determined my selfless brother would want me to do it. The second day was the longest, one hundred fifteen miles, and the toughest with a headwind out of the south. A much needed energy boost came when I came upon a golf course on the route and felt a spiritual presence. I had enjoyed some wonderful times golfing with both my brother and my father, who died in 1972. Suddenly, I was aware they were both with me, supporting me, helping me. Reenergized, I jokingly said aloud, "Okay, Bob and Dad, you two get in a quick nine holes; and I'll meet you at the end of the ride."

Recently, a prison minister friend was sharing her testimony at a monthly meeting at a Florida penitentiary. Her husband had been killed in a motorcycle accident, about a year before; and she shared that she truly believed he was now her guardian angel. We are indeed blessed by a loving Father who orchestrates both guidance and protection for us through His many assistants. But we cannot ordinarily be aware of such helpful presence if our focus is mostly on the things of this world and this physical life.

Just earlier this year, I was on another bicycle ride with Bike Florida, an organized, week-long, cross-state ride in which I've participated since 1994. An optional loop was mapped, including the town of Cassadaga, reputed to be a center for spiritualists. Though over the past year and a half, I have studied more in the spiritual realm, I don't consider myself a spiritualist; and, even today, as I am often aware of angelic presence, I don't seek continuous communication with other than the Father. By, I believe, His guidance, He has always been and remains my focus for that which is beyond this world. I also believe, when I am helped by the angels assigned to me, if I thank the Father, they are gratified. I further believe, as taught by some, that we each have a minimum of two angels assigned to us. Again, if our only focus is the physical or material, we probably aren't aware of them.

Cassadaga, is only a half hour drive from my home; but I had never been sufficiently motivated to visit. With the opportunity afforded by Bike Florida '99, I decided this would be a fun way to see the sights of this town considered spooky by some. Though we often ride in groups, I happened to be alone on this part of the ride. Approaching the town, I expected to see a lot of advertising for palm reading and the like but found that to be far less than anticipated. I found, instead, a quaint seemingly historic, small town and felt very peaceful and happy as I cycled into the town center, a crossroads of a through road with the main street of the town.

I seemed drawn by an old, white building with a long front porch with railing and banisters. Though early in the day, it was already hot; and I was ready for a rest stop. I saw a book store sign at one section of the building and had the immediate thought of air conditioning if I was fortunate enough that it be open this early. It was; and, after securing my bicycle, I gratefully entered. Refreshed by the cool air, I browsed the shelves and was surprised and pleased at the Godly content of many of the books offered. A woman nearby seemed to be an employee; and I asked the whereabouts of a restroom. A woman standing next to her remarked, "You have many high spirits with you." I simply smiled and headed for the restroom.

On return, I sought the woman who had volunteered the surprising complement and asked her if she was referring to spirits from the Celestial Heavens which she affirmed. We dialogued several minutes before my leaving to resume the Bike Florida route. As I pedaled out of Cassadaga, I was rejoicing, praising God aloud for the great blessing of the encounter with the woman who was a student medium. Suddenly, an awareness came to me and I asked, "Father, was she an angel sent by you to bless me?" The immediate response, "Well, she was all in white; wasn't she?" I almost fell off my bicycle. Indeed, she had been wearing white slacks and a white blouse but not a uniform, at least of any worldly vocation.

A Matter of Focus

I share this story as I have now shared most of my life with you, yes, in obedience to God; but I am aware of what He is doing with this work; and I am privileged to be so used to spread His good news among His children. Perhaps, you will find something here to relate to or something that will touch your *Internal Bible* to reveal the truth. All of us on this planet are on the same journey, on this road of physical life, which gives us all individuality and also gives us challenges to mold us and prepare us for what is to come. We are each given the choice of how we will react to our challenges. Will we respond by focusing on the challenge using science or religion or other people to overcome; or will we continue our unaffected focus on Father God, trusting Him to provide all our solutions?

The fact that Jesus did the latter, over and over again, isn't there just for us to admire but to emulate. That is the way our burden is easy and our yoke light. That is the way we overcome and are set free and are reborn to eternal life. That is the way of the one who is the way and the truth and the life. That is the way of love.

Love is the Way

It is all about love! Everything Jesus said, everything he did, was about love. And, when he was most severely tested, as the moment of his arrest was near, his fear so intense it manifested in sweating blood, still he focused on the Father, the will of the Father, that he never abandon the truth. The Divine Love of the Father, living in Jesus, gave him the strength to persevere.

To me, his greatest victory over self was in the garden, before his arrest, when he surrendered totally to the truth. At that moment he became an impregnable mountain of a man. No, it was not, as we have discussed earlier, the will of the Father that he suffer the cross. The will of the Father was that he stand for the truth at any cost; and the cost happened to be the cross, imposed by the enemies of the truth.

Likewise, with you and me the truth cannot be compromised. The truth is the truth, naked, not to be clothed with the embellishments of man. That the absolute truth be preserved is worth any cost we may face on this earth; for, if we compromise, our vision will become clouded; and we will eventually face the disharmony of that compromise.

While writing this book, I have been sorely tempted on more than one occasion to scrap the whole project as I am facing the possibility of isolation from many loved ones in my family, my church, and my brothers and sisters, in prison and recovery ministries, who will mistakenly see me as a traitor to Christianity. But God has persisted in returning me to this keyboard, every morning, and blessing me with the same unmistakable peace I have experienced, every time, when studying His truth and sharing His truth in both oral and written forms.

Most recently, last night, as I watched the season opener of "Touched By an Angel," I was deeply touched by the struggle of the main character, between satisfying her constituents, helping her voters through compromise, or seizing the opportunity to answer her calling to a far more worthy though unpopular cause in a far away land. Only the uncompromising truth of Jesus in his command that we must love one another gives us any chance for world peace. Only love is powerful enough to overcome the greed and tyranny of unenlightened man and cause the brotherly love of Christ to blanket the earth. This is the true second coming we all await; and, praise God, it has been initiated through the earlier referenced Padgett messages (www.divine.org) from Jesus, early in this twentieth century.

Freedom or Bondage, Our Choice

As we approach the new millennium, year 2001, there is much concern over Y2K, year 2000, misidentified as the new millennium and right around the corner from this writing. In addition to concern over approaching computer glitches, many are preaching that *Bible* prophesy is being fulfilled in natural disasters, the coming of Armageddon, the Rapture, and other prophesy. If we are walking in love, we have nothing to fear. If we are truly born again in the Essence of God, we can welcome whatever comes. Jesus in Padgett relates that his prophesy in the New Testament referred to the destruction of Jerusalem about 70 AD. The end of the world in the near future? Perhaps. We don't need God's help to destroy it ourselves; and we will if we continue to ignore Him. We do need His help to save it and to allow Him to remake it in His image working through us. Procrastination and laziness and diversion in our focus on our blessed duty to love can only result in the demise of the human race as we know it.

The Only Freedom

True, you and I and every person on earth and in the spirit world will one day know and be set free by the truth. The New Heaven of which Jesus spoke has been established with his rebirth as the first of many divine sons and daughters of God. The New Earth awaits the overcoming of humankind's stubborn refusal to see the truth, to come out of living in the dark ages of religious myth and the new age of scientism and face the reality that God loves every one of us, lovingly created each soul, condemns none of us, and anxiously awaits the day that we turn to Him, as the whole world, and lovingly pray, "Father, make us one!"

I experienced synchronicity this very morning of the day of final editing of this last chapter of *The Man in the Desert*. I watched a video tape of a popular network news program which aired last night. I had no idea of the contents of the show's three segments; but the last segment was about a woman who is both a professor and a psychiatrist. She also suffers from manic depression. Like me, she has experienced the pit of desperation to the point of attempted suicide. Her approach to overcoming her problem and similar problems with others, through her influence as a teacher, is a perfect example of scientism, at least, based on her television presentation. Science was the only consideration with not the slightest hint of past, present , or future spiritual approach to her problem. As I looked into the face and eyes of this woman, as she agreed with the pronouncement of her interviewer that she would be "dead" without her lithium medication, I saw hopelessness and dormancy of spirit. Though her condition is controlled with chemicals, she is not any more free than the addict who learns to control his compulsions. Always hovering is the possible return of the nightmare.

Please, Father, some how, some way, get this information to her heart, either through this book or religion or though one of Your angels. The professor-psychiatrist will remain in her prison until, in this world or the next, through her choice alone, she turns to the only true Source of freedom from every earthly bondage.

How Many Lives Per Soul

I stated, earlier, that Jesus in Padgett refuted reincarnation. Well, I had an experience, in the late eighties, that caused me to believe that I had lived a past life. In Chapter Two, I related that this was a particularly unhappy, desperate time in my life. One Friday evening, when I was early for a movie, I found a bookstore near the theater and decided to browse. I felt drawn to a book entitled Dianetics by L. Ron Hubbard. The book had an initial positive affect on my attitude and led me to join the Church of Scientology; and I became involved in their courses and methods.

Of particular interest was their technique of auditing. It was similar to hypnosis but a method of reliving past experiences related to problems in my life. It was to have the effect of showing me, that my mind had blown what I had perceived as flaws in my personality out of perspective, and thus help to overcome guilt and the problem itself. The concept was, if I did enough auditing, enough reliving of past experiences, I could overcome all guilt and all my problems and become a "clear" which, I suppose, would be Scientology's version of someone born again. Well, the method did nothing to help my addiction. If anything, the addiction worsened because my guilt over defiling women in my mind was temporarily decreased. It did help me with some work-related problems and did allow me to make some more clear-minded decisions that improved my career in the investment business.

In the auditing sessions I had a guide, who would assist me in becoming restful and in traveling back in my mind to past experiences, to not only remember but relive. The guide, by the way, professed to be a clear. It would seem, that in each session, I would go back further in time until, in one session, I seemed to be in a place of darkness, warmth, and comfort. All was quiet and peaceful until I heard a swishing sound. It gradually grew louder; and then there was a bright flash of light; and I realized I had experienced my own conception.

Abortion

This is one reason I have steadfastly been anti-abortion, pro-life, because, in my own experience, real or imagined, my human soul was present and incarnated at my conception. Certainly today, science tells us that experiences of a pregnant woman, even early in pregnancy, can be sensed by the baby and have profound mental affect on the child. Though Jesus in Padgett doesn't indicate when the soul enters the embryo, he does state that every soul is eager to be incarnated. This would appear to be consistent with my experience. I believe, if we assume other than the human soul's incarnation at conception, we are playing God. If this is so, abortion of a human embryo or fetus is, indeed, the killing of a human being.

It is further my belief that pro-life also means anti-death penalty. Given the eyes of Jesus, as stated earlier, I have been blessed to see the phenonominal value of every human being regardless of looks or past acts. Tie to this Jesus in Padgett relating that our time on earth is our most important time in our progress toward the Father; and we can confirm that spiritual rehabilitation, helping to change a heart for crime into a heart of love, is far more important than punishment.

In a later auditing session, I believed I had a past-life experience, or almost. Again, as in the beginning of the conception experience, I was not in body. I seemed to be in a town over a boardwalk in the early west; and I observed a man lying face down, having recently been murdered. The detail of this vision was extraordinary as he was wearing gray wool, close fitting pants with a light stripe. He had a black, leather vest over an off-white, full-sleeved shirt. A flat-top, black cowboy hat was draped down his back with the holder cord around his neck. I believed this dead body had been me. I later wondered if this explained why I was uncomfortable, in this life, wearing anything around my neck or tight-fitting collars; and, also why, in my youth, I had been so fascinated with cowboys.

About a year later, I asked my psychologist-counselor what he thought of my auditing experiences. His only comment was, "The human imagination is very powerful." I accepted his comment as, indeed, Scientology had done nothing to help me overcome my addiction which is the reason I was seeking his help. I had pretty much dead-filed the whole Scientology experience until now as, I believe, the Father has brought it to mind for this work. While I had assumed the dead body was mine, I believe the assumption was fueled by the previous witness of others experiencing past lives and my desire, at the time, to have a similar experience.

I, now, have reason to believe all such experiences result from our souls' creation before our bodies are conceived by our biological parents. Jesus in Padgett doesn't divulge how long before, only that the spirit world is filled with unincarnated souls. Since I also have come to believe that the spirit world is not separated from our earth by geography or distance but by dimension, and that human spirits are able to observe our earthly lives, I have no problem accepting that unincarnated souls may also observe us, perhaps for a long time before their incarnation. Jesus in Padgett does relate that time and space are no barriers to spirits.

Perhaps we have existed for many centuries and witnessed the lives of many souls incarnated before us. Perhaps from recollections of these past lives, not ours, man has developed the theory of reincarnation erroneously as is also true with some of his other religious and secular beliefs as earlier presented. According to Jesus in Padgett, a human soul, once entering a physical body and spirit body, however briefly, has fulfilled the purpose of incarnation which is to receive individuality. What a cruel game it would be to reincarnate a soul, over and over again, for the purpose of, each time, gaining a little more perfection until we qualify for heaven. When we understand that probation does not end with the human physical life, there is no longer need for reincarnation. I find the concept of probation and growth continuing after physical death, as spirit, far more reasonable and far more attributable to a loving Father God. In addition, as presented, we cannot qualify for residence in the highest heavens, the Celestial Heavens of the Padgett Messages, God's abode. It is only attained through God's response to our heart-felt desire and prayer, which we have identified as spiritual rebirth, again, consistent with Jesus message to Nicodemus in the *Bible*.

Probation After Death?

The *Bible* tells us death and, then, the judgment but makes no reference to the time between the two but does give reference to probation, after earthly life, in Jesus teaching about the sin against the Holy Spirit, not being forgiven either in this world or the next, inferring there is forgiveness in the next. In Padgett, he clarifies the sin against the Holy Spirit as the refusal to receive the Divine Love Essence of the Father; and the only unforgiveness involved is that such soul cannot enter the domain of the divine, again reasonable, as a spirit filled with evil or not immortal would be even more uncomfortable and tormented, surrounded by the divine, than he would be in hell. Though to a lesser degree, the discomfort would also exist for the not-transformed good spirit of the spirit world heaven. Jesus in Padgett refers to like attracting like which is true on this earth as well.

According to the theory of Houston Smith expressed at the World Community for Christian Meditation Conference in 1999, when Paul traveled to the third heaven, the information revealed to him, which he dared not reveal on earth, was that all are forgiven which is consistent with Jesus in Padgett relating that all are destined for either the spirit world heaven or the Celestial Heavens of the Father. Mr. Smith speculated that Paul feared such revelation on earth would cause people to run amok without moral control. Jesus in Padgett elaborates that though the Father has no unforgiveness, each sin carries its own penalty which will be exacted, again, referring to the Biblical as we sow we reap.

Transformation Not Atonement

Thus there is a hell of darkness and torment, spirit spheres, occupied by souls entering the spirit world in the condition which is out of harmony with God's immutable laws. There, penalties are exacted and only as souls suffer and repent do they gradually come into the light and out of their torment. The chapter on heaven and hell elaborates further on this issue and this information is only repeated that the third man may be confident that there is truly nothing to fear in leaving this life unless he has been out of harmony with God's laws. If so, then he is better of for having received this information now, as this could prove a key time in initiating his repentance and seeking rebirth in the Divine Love of the Father, seeking transformation not atonement though the sacrifice of another.

I remind the reader also that it is not the blood of Jesus appeasing an angry god that washes our sins; but, rather, it is being reborn through the Holy Spirit in the Divine Love that transforms us into new creatures thereby cleansing our souls and creating a oneness with the Father wherein we are no longer like Him in image only but also in substance. His Divine Presence in our souls will, in His time, cause our final transformation into the Divine Angel. What a glorious future our all-loving Father makes available to us if we will but seek it. Rebirth is real. Transformation is real. I have experienced both after having been lost in addiction and religious myth all of my adult life to age fifty. This work is a testament to the wonderful benevolence of our loving Creator Father.

All About Love

Also the premise that we are saved by faith that Jesus of Nazareth is God or by any faith is totally false. Nothing we do saves us. Paul in the *Bible* stated that if we have faith without love, we have nothing. This is the truth. I repeat, it is all about love! Jesus in Padgett, speaking about rebirth, states that faith comes after receiving the Divine Love of the Father, the kind of faith that transformed his apostles from ignorant, doubting, greedy cowards into almost clones of him. Again, Paul in the *Bible* relates that we will be like Jesus which he was addressing to the born again. As Divine Angels, we will indeed be like him.

You may say, "Well, what about the heart-felt desire that the human must express to the Father before the Father responds with His Divine Love delivered by His Holy Spirit? Doesn't the desire and sincerity come before we receive the love." Yes, true, but what is the root of the desire? Again, our love for God, inferior as it is in comparison to His perfect, Divine Love, is the trigger to our desire. And seeing His awesome, everyday love for us is the trigger to our love for Him. It is all about love!

This is what Jesus meant when he said we will know the truth and the truth will set us free. When I made that first forty day journey in the desert of my soul, God's love for me gave the response to my prayer of desperation; day-by-day, I expressed my love and desire for God; God sent His Holy Spirit to imbue my soul with His Divine Love; with my rebirth my vision changed so radically I thought this must be the way Jesus saw the world; I saw the truth; my forty year compulsion disappeared as if it had never existed; I would never again be comfortable in sin.

There is no other spiritual or religious experience which compares with being born again which gives such dramatic evidence of God's existence. If one merely thinks he has been born again, he is not, as this experience is absolutely known and is the only way to the Celestial Heavens. Some may profess to be born again or saved because of a great emotional experience; but emotion does not confirm rebirth. Only transformation does, again, as so stated by Paul in the *Bible*.

This is not exclusively for Christians but inclusive of all of God's children through Jesus, as the Christ, as the Divine Love, which is the way, the truth, the life. Remember, always, God does not require that we be one hundred percent correct, just one hundred percent sincere in our desire for Him. Yet, if we are not, He will not punish us. He will help us to hone our natural love to the perfection of the heaven of the spirit world where our soul progression is limited but our joy and peace continue to grow in harmony with His laws.

Why this restating from an earlier chapter, though in different words? First, because I am obedient; and I am not writing my own words in my own plan. True, God is drawing on my life experience to communicate a living, true parable to you; but He is the director of this work, what is to be said and where in the book it is to be said. He wants you to know that the opportunity to choose rebirth, though the event is administered by Him, by His Holy Spirit, is the greatest gift given to you as a human being and is the ultimate purpose for another great gift, your *Internal Bible*.

God wants you to know that any person or teacher or clergy that disputes this is living or teaching a lie; and, though He is a loving, benevolent God, He does not violate His own laws and is not, as the *Bible* sometimes portrays Him, a hypocrite. Those who live or teach lies are out of harmony with His immutable laws and will only know His light and His heavens after coming back into harmony through the ways He provides as earlier discussed. It's all about love!

Reason

Again, the reference to the quote from Pope John Paul II at the beginning of this work: "Faith and reason are like two wings on which the human spirit rises to the contemplation of truth." Faith does not have to be unreasonable. Reasoning added to my faith, from the study of the Padgett Messages and other similar works spanning the last three centuries of communication between residents of the spirit world, God's angels, and mortals, has removed all my fear and concern of what awaits my loved ones beyond this life, including a daughter who professes to be an agnostic. And, is it not reasonable that God, who the *Bible* defines as love, would want us to live without such fear?

I now have understanding and empathy for my agnostic daughter; and I admit to a resentment I feel toward the church that brainwashed me in man-made dogmas of superstition and manipulation. My resentment is not directed at any specific persons; and I have no desire to research the responsibility for the myths. I can feel only pity for the souls who so manipulated the truth and regret for the darkness they must experience.

I am grateful to be asked and equipped, through my life experience, to expose the truth, which I hope will set many free and further enlighten those already free, including you the reader of this copy. Any person, by combining reason with his faith, can and eventually will, according to Jesus in Padgett, see that the dogmas of a man-god or god-man, or atonement by blood sacrifice of anybody or anything, or salvation by faith without transformation are unreasonable, false, and grossly misleading.

Evolution of the Church

Initially, I was concerned, when I read Jesus' prophesy in Padgett, that the Catholic Church and its priests will lose their power. I believe the Church has changed more toward love since the time of that prophesy, early in this century; but, I fear, it has not changed enough for Pope John Paul II or his eventual replacement to accept this message. I truly love and respect the current Pope and regard him a great leader. His courage in standing for the morality taught by our savior is a living example that the truth cannot be compromised. I believe he is seeing more of the truth as evidenced by his recent refuting of hell as a place of eternal fire and brimstone and his reference to Purgatory, rarely mentioned today, even among Catholics, which speaks to the truth of probation after physical death.

In addition, the Pope has declared 1999 as a year of focus on God the Father which, I believe, is no accident. I can only hope and pray that he will favorably receive at least some of what is presented in this work. Whether he receives and accepts but, then, acts to institute change is quite another thing which can be prayed for by all Christians who see truth here. I say all Christians, as he truly is an ecumenical Pope, who represents all Christians before the secular, immoral world. In my opinion as a Catholic Christian, the Church is most lacking in its understanding of true rebirth and its teaching thereon.

The Future of Organized Religion

Change is necessary in many areas if Christian churches are to survive. The Catholic mass, by focusing on the atonement and the worship of Jesus as God, is an abomination which perpetuates false doctrine in the souls of worshippers. Thanks to God's benevolence, I believe, the worship and prayers of many do get through to Him. But how much better if the celebration of the mass was focused on truth instead of myth originated long before Christianity was born?

The Catholic Church is not alone in perpetuating the errors of man with some other churches to a greater degree in their exclusive, unbending fundamentalism and some to a lesser degree, especially some of the interdenominational churches, but still professing false dogma. If I were guiding a new Christian in finding a church today, I would probably suggest one more focused on rebirth through the Holy Spirit than on Eucharist and more focused on worshipping the Father than Jesus, love-filled, joy-filled, rejecting none, respecting and loving all God's children. Or I would recommend an ecumenical fellowship, focused on the expression of God's love to the underprivileged of society and the world, which may provide a more rewarding, closer experience with God than an organized church which has been my experience with prison ministry. Through such ministries of agape love, is this not the fulfillment of St. John's expression that "he, who lives in love, lives in God and God in him" and Jesus' command in the *Bible* that we must love each other as he loved us?

For myself, I plan to remain a member of the Roman Catholic Church as long as it allows, while it exists, and I am alive on earth. I feel this is my direction from God, that I seek opportunities, both within the church and without, to participate in activities that allow me to share and fellowship. I would likewise counsel other church members, of all denominations, who accept the teaching of this work as truth, to not leave their churches, if their churches are love oriented but, instead, to endeavor to spread the truth from within, without being imposing. Jesus in Padgett expresses we do not have to fully agree with the doctrine of a church to participate in worship. We do not, in my opinion, need more denominations but more true Christianity within our existing denominations. Those churches, which refuse to evolve toward the truth, will, in accordance with Jesus' prophesy, become non-entities.

Freedom Ministers

God has given me a vision for a Freedom Retreat Center to train freedom ministers to become His emissaries of love and truth and the resulting freedom to the world. People from all denominations and all religions or without organized religious experience will be welcomed. Yes, we will even welcome agnostics and atheists, who are willing to learn, as they are also God's beloved children destined for heaven.

Jesus in Padgett stated that the truths disclosed in those key fifty-two messages can be accepted by all major religions without people changing from their traditions. Indeed, I believe this was the reason God has brought me to an awareness and appreciation for Houston Smith and the treasures of his mind, heart, and pen, which I have only started to study and which, I anticipate, may lead to another work from this author. Anyone interested in participating in the formation of the Freedom Retreat Center can contact me through the *Freedom Ministries Inc*. web site (www.40days2freedom.org) which provides an e-mail link.

God's Harmony

The religious leaders of the past and the present have much to account for. As to the evolution of their manipulation, the ignorance of those in the present will not be accepted as an exonerating excuse. When we are out of harmony with God's laws, the only exoneration is to come back into harmony, admitting the falsities created by man and seeking only the truth. This lack of harmony with God, I believe, is the primary reason so many priests today find their vocation intolerable. The exodus from the clergy from all organized churches, specified earlier, is staggering. As the years pass, they grow uncomfortable with the faith dictated by their churches. Many rebel and leave their vocations often not knowing why or blaming burnout or sexual temptation. Among Catholic priests, celibacy would be less an issue if they were truly comfortable with their faith; but they fight to ignore their *Internal Bible*s which will not give them rest while they live a lie.

So we come back now to you, the third man or woman. What do you now see? How do you feel? In harmony? Enlightened? Reborn? Angry? At whom? Me? Your church? If you have read this entire work, I confess, regardless of your answers, I am pleased as, I believe, some day, you will remember what you have read here and realize it is the truth. This remembrance, this awareness, will make your journey back to your Creator Father easier and more sure; and you will be more likely, whether in this life or as a pure spirit, to seek His most awesome gift, His Divine Love Essence, and the ultimate transformation into the Divine Angel. Thus, I am pleased; and our Father is pleased. Amen.

ACKNOWLEDGEMENTS

The following works and individuals have blessed and inspired this author and have helped him to grow in knowledge, spiritual awareness, and closeness to God and our brother Jesus and have thereby contributed to this work. The listings are in no particular order. A listing does not indicate this author's total acceptance of all material presented but rather spiritual enrichment or stimulation from the overall work. All references to information in the *Bible* in this work are recalled from memory and can therefore be considered as paraphrased. Though there is no reference to *Bible* book, chapter, or verse, the reader may research references through the use of a concordance.

The Internal Bible, Father God, the foundation of subconscious knowledge and truth about God initiated in our souls at their creation to provide guidance for our journey home.

The Shroud of Turin, the Gospel of Jesus, written by Jesus and his Father using no mortal hand; images in *The Man in the Desert* courtesy of Russ Breault, Founder of the Shroud of Turin Education Project, Inc. (www.shroud2000.com);

The Holy Bible, various versions, the Old Testament books of Psalms, Genesis, Job, and Jonah and all of the books of the New Testament with the exception of Revelation;

40 Days to Freedom, by this author, continues to bless me daily though completed seven years ago, both traditional and contemporary spirituality some of which the author had virtually no knowledge before the writing;

The Celestial Testament of Jesus, Jesus the Christ, using the human instruments James E. Padgett and Leslie R. Stone, web site (www.divine.org) by Victor Summers; other than the Shroud, the most important work to this author in exposing the myths of Christianity and the truths that Jesus actually taught (thanks, Vic!);

Spirit Teachings, William S. Moses, (library at www.divine.org) an education on spirit communications with those of this world and a nineteenth century harbinger of *The Celestial Testament of Jesus*;

Angelic Messages to All, Sister Carolyn and Brother Michael, web site (www.angelicmessages.org);

Light in My Darkness, The Story of My Life, Helen Keller, she saw better than most and what she saw filled her heart with joy (thanks, George!);

Masterpieces of American Indian Literature, Willis G. Regier, including *The Life of Kahgegagahbowh* by George Copway, *The Soul of the Indian* by Charles Eastman, *American Indian Stories* by Zitkala-Sa, and *Black Elk Speaks* as told to John G. Neihardt; their example of harmony with God and His creation remains the envy of this author;

Although The Fig Tree Shall Not Blossom, Daena Cargnel, the autobiography of a woman pastor;

Desire of Ages, E. G. White, a beautiful chronography of the life of Jesus based on the *Bible* (thanks, Dick!);

Around the World in 80 Years, the story of Arthur Burt, evangelist;

Living *in the Light of Eternity*; K. P. Yohannan, a Christian author, born and raised in India;

The God We Never Knew, Marcus J. Borg, presents a mature contemporary view of Christianity and discloses sources of some of its myths;

The Celestine Vision, James Redfield, wonderful perception of meaningful coincidence called synchronicity plus explanation of the relationship of matter and energy and the human psyche;

The Blood and the Shroud, Jesus: the Evidence, The Shroud of Turin, Ian Wilson, wonderful works from a thorough researcher drawn to Christianity through his work;

Divine Guidance, Doreen Virtue, tuning in to God and His helpers;

The DNA of God?, Dr. Leoncio A. Garza-Valdes, analysis of the ancient blood on the Shroud of Turin;

Grace Walk, Steve McVey, instead of working for God, allowing God to work through us;

Our Spiritual Resources, Joel S. Goldsmith, to read and reread (thanks, Blair!);

A Simple Path, Mother Teresa, who was perhaps the greatest human expression of unselfish love in the twentieth century (thanks, Patsy!);

Emolition: The Essential Experience Beyond Coping, Jim Wilson and John Gossett, Jim was my final professional counselor for my addiction and the most helpful of human resources (thanks, Jimmy!);

Partners in Prayer, John Maxwell, the power of group and individual and intercessory prayer;

A Portrait of Jesus, *Joshua*, Joseph E. Girzone, a Catholic priest devoted to the pursuit of truth;

Confessions of a Catholic Worker, Michael O. Garvey, great and true word picture of daily life at a home for the homeless;

No Wonder They Call Him the Savior, Max Lucado, the passion and cross of Jesus (thanks, Steve!);

The Imitation of Christ, Thomas A. Kempis, a basic work on Christianity;

Discover the Power Within You, Eric Butterworth, great exploration of the inner person;

The Mind of Christ, T. W. Hunt, how to focus on God;

Portrait of Jesus?, Frank C. Tribbe, one of the earliest books on the Shroud of Turin Research Project of 1977 to 1983;

Augustine Day by Day, John E. Rotelle, O.S.A., minute daily meditations from the writings of St. Augustine;

The Cloud of Unknowing, anonymous fourteenth century author, a foundation for meditation and contemplative prayer;

The Practice of the Presence of God, Brother Lawrence of the Resurrection, how to be consciously aware of God's presence all the time from one who was (thanks, George!);

Living Light, Kenneth N. Taylor, morning and evening selections from The Living *Bible*;

The Seven Story Mountain (thanks, Patty!), *The Wisdom of the Desert* (thanks, Blair!), *The Monastic Journey, The Sign of Jonas*, *Disputed Questions*, *No Man is an Island*,

Contemplation in a World of Action, Thomas Merton, other than Jesus, my favorite human author;

ENCYCLICAL LETTER OF THE SUPREME PONTIFF JOHN PAUL II TO THE BISHOPS OF THE CATHOLIC CHURCH ON THE RELATIONSHIP BETWEEN FAITH AND REASON, *Crossing the Threshold of Hope*, Pope John Paul II, defender of life;

The Human Spirit in the Third Millennium: Return to the Light, Huston Smith, The John Main Seminar 1999, World Community for Christian Meditation, Laurence Freeman OSB; Huston Smith is a national treasure;

Multidisciplinary Investigation of an Enigma, Shroud of Turin Conference, Shroud of Turin Center at Mary Mother of the Church Abbey, Richmond, Virginia, June 18 - 20, 1999;

The International Holy Shroud Guild Seminar-Retreat, Mount Saint Alphonsus, Esopus, New York, August 23 - 25, 1996;

Special thanks to the board members of Freedom Ministries, Inc., for their prayers and support, especially for this work: Jody, Bill, Tom, and George. Also, special thanks to daughter Peggy for her love and editing talents and Jerry for the publishing information.

I also greatfully acknowledge the guidance and inspiration of Father God in this work and in my life.

Thank you, Father, for removing the scales from my eyes that I may see with the eyes of Jesus. Thank You for Your sustinence that I was able to focus only on You and Your holy work in this ministry and in this project. Thank You, most of all, for Your Holy Spirit and Divine Love through which all Your chidren in Your image are allowed to become one with You in substance thus sharing in Your divinity. And thank You for sending Your son, Jesus, not to die on the cross but to show us Your way, Your truth, Your Life. Thank You, Father, for being all about love. Amen

ABOUT THE AUTHOR

Tom Lomas was born and raised in New England and by all appearances, experienced a normal childhood. After graduating cum laude from Worcester Junior College, he embarked on a career as a flying officer in the Air Force and married the girl of his dreams whom he met while training in Central Florida. While still in his twenties, an incident exposed his addiction and resulted in psychiatric counseling. A year later, Tom's military career was terminated and his family of five, soon to be six, was thrust into civilian life.

He succeeded in sales to the extent, within a few years, the Lomas family, in the eyes of the world, was better off than had they remained in the military. Though a Catholic Christian all his life, in 1972, Tom experienced a spiritual awakening which would be the cornerstone for his future spiritual growth. For the next ten years, the children grew to young adulthood and the Lomases appeared to be living the good life in Central Florida, and then, Tom's addiction again raised its ugly head to be noticed. This resulted in the end of a twenty-three year marriage and Tom's failed suicide attempt.

As with *Dr. Jekyll and Mr. Hyde*, the monster within gained more and more control. Tom again sought professional help, but, as in the past, self control was short lived. He again turned to suicide as resolution but made a final desperate prayer for help to the One he saw as his last resort. The prayer was answered with a procedure which resulted in a total healing. Tom was then influenced to write a book about the procedure so others with similar afflictions could receive the same healing.

In the ensuing years Tom would become involved in prison ministry, form Freedom Ministries, Inc., a non-profit, charitable institution and give away more than sixteen thousand hard copies of *40 Days to Freedom* throughout the USA and twenty-three other countries. *The Freedom Lettter*, also authored by Tom, has shared written testimonies of healing from all sorts of addiction, obsession, and depression from all over the world.

In early 1999, Tom was inspired to write his second book, *The Man in the Desert*, which would provide the same freedom as the first and so much more.

www.ingramcontent.com/pod-product-compliance
Lightning Source LLC
Chambersburg PA
CBHW030439290526
45786CB00001B/355